Crystal Reports XI

Level 1

Chris Blocher

Crystal Reports XI: Level 1

Part Number: 085517
Course Edition: 1.01

Acknowledgments

Project Team

Content Developer: Chris Blocher • **Content Manager:** Cheryl Russo • **Graphic Designer:** Alex Tong • **Project Coordinator:** Liz Timm • **Content Editor:** Margaux Phillips • **Material Editor:** Andrew Lowe • **Business Matter Expert and Technical Reviewer:** Drew Fierst • **Project Technical Support:** Mike Toscano

NOTICES

HELP US IMPROVE OUR COURSEWARE

Your comments are important to us. Please contact us at Element K Press LLC, 1-800-478-7788, 500 Canal View Boulevard, Rochester, NY 14623, Attention: Product Planning, or through our Web site at **http://support.elementkcourseware.com**.

CRYSTAL REPORTS XI: LEVEL 1

Contents

LESSON 5: FORMATTING REPORTS

LESSON 6: ENHANCING REPORTS

CONTENTS

ABOUT THIS COURSE

Crystal Reports XI: Level 1 is the primary recommended course you should take if your job responsibilities require you to obtain output from databases. It is also the first course in the Crystal Reports XI series. In this course, you will build basic list and group reports that work with almost any database.

Information is critical to making sound business decisions. However, too much data or information presented in a manner that has no meaning has little or no value. By using Crystal Reports, you can build reports that extract and summarize the data you need and present the data so that it is meaningful to you and others who view those reports.

Course Description

Target Student

This course is designed for a person who needs output from a database. In some cases, database programs have limited reporting tools, and/or they may not have access to those tools. Students may or may not have programming and/or SQL experience.

Course Prerequisites

Before taking this course, students should be familiar with the basic functions of Windows, such as creating and navigating folders, opening programs, manipulating windows, copying and pasting objects, formatting text, and saving files. In addition, students should have taken *Microsoft® Office Access 2003: Level 1* or have equivalent experience with basic database concepts.

How to Use This Book

As a Learning Guide

Each lesson covers one broad topic or set of related topics. Lessons are arranged in order of increasing proficiency with *Crystal Reports XI*; skills you acquire in one lesson are used and developed in subsequent lessons. For this reason, you should work through the lessons in sequence.

We organized each lesson into results-oriented topics. Topics include all the relevant and supporting information you need to master *Crystal Reports XI*, and activities allow you to apply this information to practical hands-on examples.

You get to try out each new skill on a specially prepared sample file. This saves you typing time and allows you to concentrate on the skill at hand. Through the use of sample files, hands-on activities, illustrations that give you feedback at crucial steps, and supporting background information, this book provides you with the foundation and structure to learn *Crystal Reports XI* quickly and easily.

As a Review Tool

Any method of instruction is only as effective as the time and effort you are willing to invest in it. In addition, some of the information that you learn in class may not be important to you immediately, but it may become important later on. For this reason, we encourage you to spend some time reviewing the topics and activities after the course. For additional challenge when reviewing activities, try the "What You Do" column before looking at the "How You Do It" column.

As a Reference

The organization and layout of the book make it easy to use as a learning tool and as an after-class reference. You can use this book as a first source for definitions of terms, background information on given topics, and summaries of procedures.

Course Objectives

In this course, you will build basic list and group reports that work with almost any database.

You will:

- create a report by using data from an existing database.
- use a report to present specific data in the desired order.
- create groups to summarize report data.
- build formulas to calculate and display data.
- format reports.
- add and modify elements in a report.
- create single data series charts.
- distribute report data.

Course Requirements

Hardware

- A Pentium II or faster processor.
- 350 MB of hard-disk space (600 MB recommended).
- 128 MB of RAM (256 MB RAM recommended).
- Access to one of the following: a local CD-ROM drive, a local DVD drive, or access to a networked CD-ROM drive.

Software

- Microsoft Windows XP, 2000 SP4, or above.
- A custom installation of Crystal Reports XI.
- A default installation of Access 2003 if you plan to complete the activity, "Exporting to an Access Database."
- A default installation of the free Adobe® Reader® 7.0 application if you plan to complete the activity, "Exporting to PDF."
- A default installation of Excel 2003 if you plan to complete the activity, "Exporting to Excel."
- A default installation of Word 2003 or newer if you plan to complete the activity, "Adding Bulleted Lists."
- A valid email address if you plan to complete the lab activity, "Enhancing a Report."

Class Setup

This course was written using Crystal Reports XI Professional Edition and Microsoft Windows XP.

1. Perform a custom installation of Crystal Reports XI.
   a. With Autoplay enabled, place the Crystal Reports XI Professional Edition CD in the computer's CD-ROM drive.
   b. On the Crystal Reports XI Setup Wizard's Welcome page, click Next.
   c. Accept the License Agreement and click Next.
   d. Enter your user information, product key code, and click Next.
   e. On the Select Installation Type page, select Custom, leave the Destination Folders as is, and click Next.
   f. On the Select Features page, click the Export Support drop-down arrow, select the Entire Feature Will Be Installed On Local Hard Drive option, and click Next.
   g. Click Next twice to begin installing Crystal Reports.
   h. If desired, register the product, or click Register Later and then click Finish.
2. If necessary, reboot your computer.
3. Install a default installation copy of Microsoft Office Access 2003, Microsoft Office Excel 2003, and Microsoft Office Word 2003.

4. Install the Adobe® Reader® 7.0.

5. On the course CD-ROM, open the 085_517 folder. Then, open the Data folder. Run the 085517dd.exe self-extracting file located within. This will install a folder named 085517Data on your C drive. This folder contains the data files you will need to complete this course.

6. This is an optional step. If data files are copied to a different folder than instructed in the Course Setup, users will receive an error message when they attempt to refresh data.

   The error can be corrected by either re-installing the data files to the appropriate folder as instructed in the previous step; or by using Crystal Reports' Set Datasource Location option to modify the location of the database files to match the installed location. To use the Set Datasource Location option:

   a. Open any Crystal Reports data file listed in the C:\085517 folder.

   b. Choose Database→Set Datasource Location. The Set Datasource Location dialog box is displayed.

   c. From the Current Data Source list, select the database or table you want to replace.

   d. From the Replace With list, select the database or table you want to use.

   e. Click Update.

   f. Repeat steps c through e as needed.

   g. Click Close to close the Set Datasource Location dialog box.

   h. Repeat steps a through g for each Crystal Reports class data file.

7. Verify that file extensions are displayed in Windows Explorer.

   a. If necessary, start Windows Explorer.

   b. To display the Folder Options dialog box, choose Tools→Folder Options.

   c. On the View tab, verify that the Hide File Extensions For Known File Types option is unchecked.

   d. Click OK and close Windows Explorer.

8. In addition to the specific setup procedures needed for this class to run properly, you should also check the Element K Press product support Web site at **http://support.elementkcourseware.com** for more information. Any updates about this course will be posted there.

List of Additional Files

Printed with each activity is a list of files students open to complete that activity. Many activities also require additional files that students do not open, but are needed to support the file(s) students are working with. These supporting files are included with the student data files on the course CD-ROM or data disk. Do not delete these files.

LESSON 1
Creating a Report

Lesson Time
1 hour(s), 30 minutes to 2 hour(s)

Lesson Objectives:

In this lesson, you will create a report by using data from an existing database.

You will:

- Set default report settings.
- Specify fields for a report.
- Preview a report.
- Change field labels and field formatting.
- Add a report title.
- Move fields in a report.
- Access additional fields by adding a table.

Introduction

Information is commonly stored in databases. At some point, you will likely want to present some of that data in a report. In this lesson, you will create a report from information in a database.

Using Crystal Reports, you can select only the data you need from databases and build a report that summarizes and presents that information in a meaningful way.

TOPIC A

Set Default Report Settings

Before you begin creating reports in Crystal Reports, you may want to customize some of the program's default settings. In this topic, you will customize several default settings.

You want your reports to use particular settings that differ from the defaults. You can customize Crystal Reports' settings so that your own settings will be used by default for every new report you create.

Crystal Reports XI

Crystal Reports XI is a program that allows you to use database information to create reports. These reports enable you to provide users with targeted information so they can analyze and interpret important information without having to sift through an entire database.

Report Considerations

When deciding on the content of a report, ask the following questions:

- Who will use the report?
- What is the report's purpose?
- What data should be included?
- How should the report be formatted?
- Does the data exist or do you need to create it?
- How should the data be filtered and sorted?
- How will the report be distributed?

Report Types

There are a number of different types of reports you can create.

Report Type	Description
List	Displays database fields in columns.
Grouped	Displays data hierarchically so that the data can be summarized.

Report Type	Description
Subreport	A report within another report.
Cross-tab	Displays data two-dimensionally with column and row headings and summarized data as the intersection, allowing you to analyze the relationship of two or more fields.
Drill-down	Displays summarized data only. The detailed data is hidden and can be viewed by drilling down.

Program Window Components

Crystal Reports includes several window components that are displayed by default.

Component	Description
Menu bar	Displays a list of commands.
Standard toolbar	Contains buttons that you can use to access common commands.
Formatting toolbar	Contains buttons that you can use to access common formatting commands.
Insert Tools toolbar	Contains buttons that you can use to access advanced, report-enhancing commands.
Expert Tools toolbar	Contains buttons that you can use to access many advanced experts.
Start Page	Displayed in the design area, it provides quick access to common tasks, such as researching Crystal Reports, creating new reports, or opening recent ones.
Status bar	A horizontal bar at the bottom of the application window that provides information regarding the current state of the report or selected object.

LESSON 1

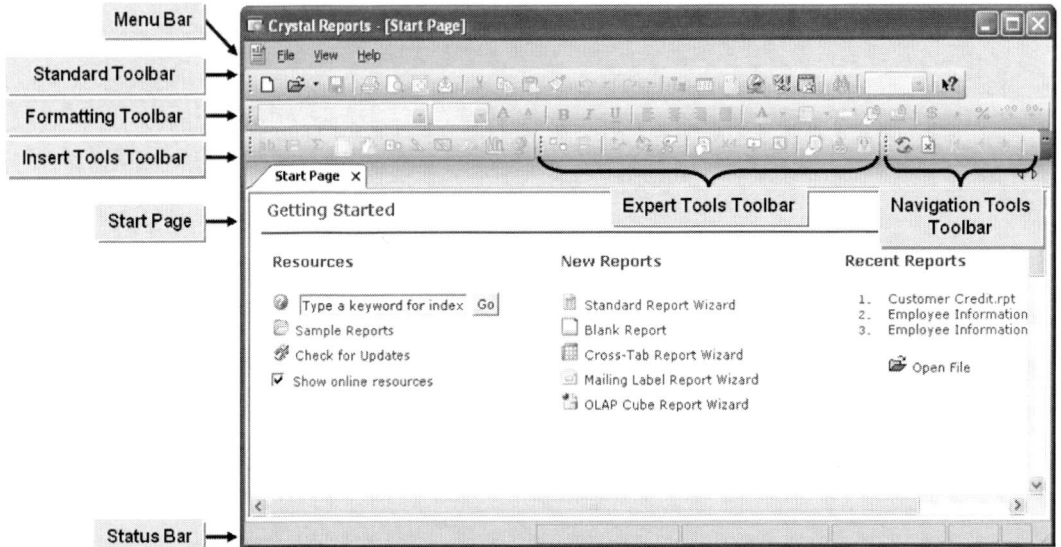

Figure 1-1: *Components of the Crystal Reports window.*

Report Area Components

Once you open a report in Crystal Reports, the environment in the report area changes. Figure 1-2 identifies some of the components you will see in the report area.

Component	Description
Design tab	The tab on which you perform most of the work when creating and modifying a report.
Preview tab	The tab used to display the database data.
Rulers	Vertical and horizontal visual references for moving and re-sizing report objects.
Guidelines	Nonprinting guides that you can place in the ruler to assist you in positioning objects.
Sections	Design areas where you can add fields and other report content.
Field	A category of information.
Field label	A label that identifies a category of information.

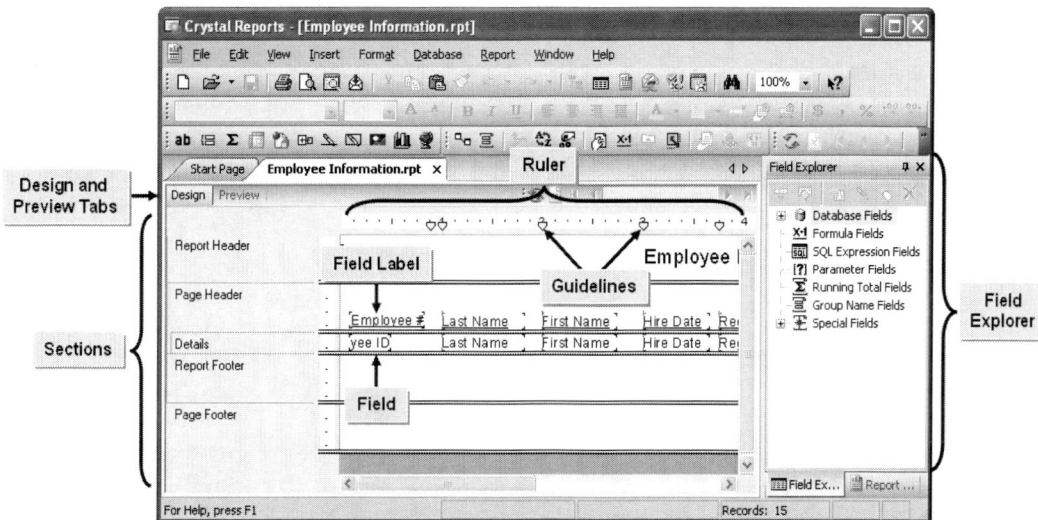

Figure 1-2: *Components in an open report.*

Workbench

As you begin creating more reports, juggling many files can become confusing. To help you organize your work, you can use the Workbench. Displayed on the right side of the program window, it enables you to arrange multiple reports into a single project for quick access. Able to display multiple projects and the reports they contain, the Workbench can be displayed or hidden by choosing View→Workbench.

Field Explorer

Crystal Reports provides the Field Explorer as a convenient way for you to work with fields in a report. Displaying a hierarchical structure of fields currently in the open report and a list of those that can be inserted into the report, the Field Explorer makes it easy to add, modify, and remove fields as needed.

Field Types

Each database contains fields. Each field has a designated data type. Formatting options will differ based on the data type.

Data Type	Description
Number	Can contain only numbers, a period for a decimal point, or a minus sign.
String	Can contain a combination of characters, including text, numbers, and symbols.
Date	Can contain a date only.
DateTime	Can contain a date, a time, or a combination of both.
Currency	Can contain numbers and avoids rounding errors, unlike the Number data type.
Boolean	Can contain data that can have a true or false value.

Tooltips and Fields

Not only can tooltips help you identify components within the Crystal Reports window, but they can also help you identify details about objects and fields. By placing the mouse pointer over a field, you can determine the table from which the field was inserted, the field name, and the field type. If a tooltip disappears, simply move the mouse pointer to a blank area of the report. Then, place the mouse pointer over the appropriate field or field label again.

Design Tab Sections

The Design tab is where you will create your reports. It contains five sections to which you can add content. Figure 1-2 shows these sections in a report.

> The Design tab contains data representations, not the actual report data, so you can perform all types of tasks without tying up the computer or network resources needed to gather the data.

Section	Function
Report Header	Displays only once at the beginning of a report and can contain items such as a title page, logo, introductory information, or charts or cross-tabs that apply to the entire report.
Page Header	Displays at the top of every page and can contain items such as field titles, print date/time, and the name of the document.
Details	Displays once per record and contains the bulk of the report data.
Report Footer	Displays only once at the end of the report and can contain items such as grand totals, charts, or cross-tabs that apply to the entire report.
Page Footer	Displays at the bottom of every page and can contain items such as page numbers and report names.

The Preview Tab

After designing a report, you can see how it will look when printed by clicking the Print Preview button on the Standard toolbar. The Preview tab is displayed to the right of the Design tab. By default, the section names on the Preview tab are abbreviated, so Report Header is abbreviated as RH on the Preview tab. Figure 1-3 displays an example of a report that is displayed on the Preview tab.

> Clicking the Print Preview button on the Standard toolbar also switches from the Design tab to the Preview tab.

> The user can control how a report's section names are displayed by choosing File→Options and selecting the desired options on the Layout tab.

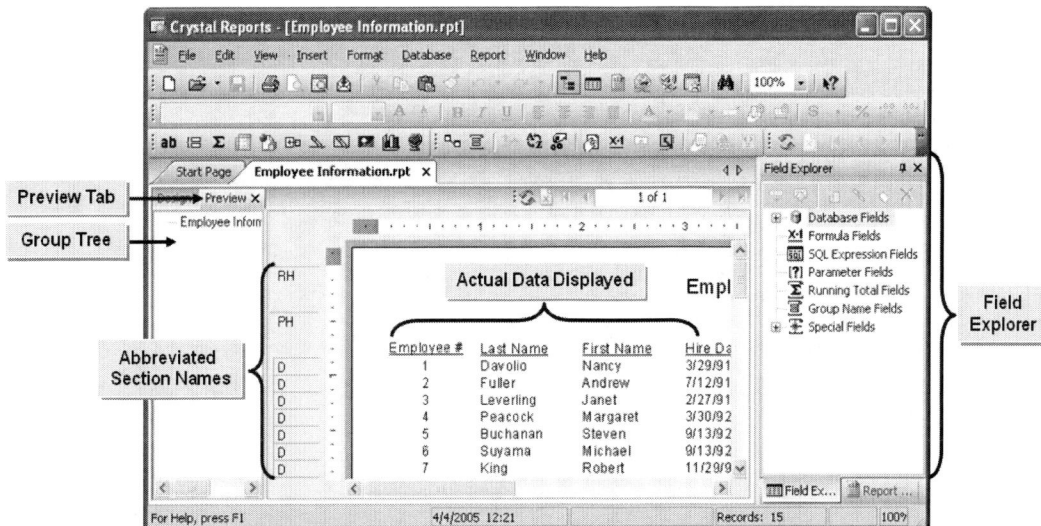

Figure 1-3: *The Preview tab displays a report's data.*

Saved Data

Crystal Reports uses the saved data until you perform an action, either refresh the report or add a new field, which requires Crystal Reports to retrieve new data.

Group Tree

When previewing a report, the Group Tree will display a hierarchical structure of groups and subgroups if the report contains any. Clicking a group or subgroup will automatically display that data in the report area.

Default Settings

Crystal Reports has two types of default settings: those that affect the behavior of all new reports and those that only affect the current report.

Setting	Description
Field Formats	**Function:** Controls the formatting for all string, number, currency, date, time, date/time, and boolean fields. **Default:** Specific to each field.
Data Source Defaults	**Function:** Controls the folder location of the data sources. **Default:** Unspecified.
Convert NULL Field Value To Default	**Function:** Converts any null field values to the database default value. **Default:** Off.
Default Fonts	**Function:** Controls the font for all fields in a report. **Default:** Arial 10.
Display Group Tree	**Function:** Creates a group tree on the left side of a grouped report. **Default:** On.
Save Data With Report	**Function:** Automatically saves data with the report. **Default:** On.
Discard Saved Data On Open	**Function:** Removes existing data from a report when opening (recommended when data is password protected). **Default:** Off.

How to Set Default Report Settings

Procedure Reference: Format Any Field Type

To change the formatting of String, Number, Currency, Date, Time, Date/Time, and Boolean fields:

1. Choose File→Options to display the Options dialog box.

2. Select the Fields tab.

3. On the Fields tab, click the button corresponding to the field type whose settings you want to change. The Format Editor dialog box for that field type is displayed.

4. Make the appropriate changes to the default settings.

   - To specify basic formatting, border, or hyperlink options for any field type, use the Common, Border, and Hyperlink tabs.

   - To specify number formatting options for Number or Currency fields, use the Number tab.

   - To specify date or time formatting options for Date or Time fields, use the Date or Time tab.

   - To specify Boolean options for Boolean fields, use the Boolean tab.

5. Click OK to close the Format Editor dialog box and return to the Fields tab of the Options dialog box.

6. Click OK to close the Options dialog box.

Procedure Reference: Change Fonts for Any Field Type

To change the fonts for any field type:

1. Choose File→Options to display the Options dialog box.

2. Select the Fonts tab.

3. Under Default Fonts, click the button corresponding to the field type whose font you want to change. The Font dialog box is displayed.

4. Make the desired changes to the default font settings for fields, summary fields, group name fields, text objects, field titles, or charts.

5. Click OK to close the Font dialog box and return to the Fonts tab of the Options dialog box.

6. Click OK to close the Options dialog box.

Procedure Reference: Change Report-Level Defaults

If you want to affect the behavior of the current report only, you can change the report options. To change report-level defaults:

1. Open the desired report.

   You can display the Open dialog box from the Start Page by choosing File→Open, by clicking the Open button on the Standard toolbar, or by pressing Ctrl+O.

2. Choose File→Report Options to display the Report Options dialog box.

3. Make the desired changes to the report's default settings.

4. Click OK to close the Report Options dialog box.

5. Save the report.

ACTIVITY **1-1**

Modifying Default Settings for Reports

Data Files:

*   Orders.rpt

Setup:

Crystal Reports and the data files have been installed as detailed in the Course Setup.

Scenario:

You recently installed Crystal Reports and you need to set some program and report defaults so that you don't have to reset them every time you create a new report.

What You Do	How You Do It
1. Open the Orders.rpt report in Crystal Reports and maximize the application.	a. Choose Start→All Programs→Business Objects 11→Crystal Reports→Crystal Reports 11.
	b. In the upper-right corner of the Workbench pane, **click the Close button.**
	c. On the Start Page, under Recent Reports, **click Open File.**
	d. **Navigate to the C:\085517Data folder.**
	e. **Select Orders.rpt and click Open.**
	f. On the Design tab, **observe the section names.** Notice that the section names are displayed fully.
2. Display the Fields tab of the Options dialog box.	a. **Choose File→Options.**
	b. In the Options dialog box, **select the Fields tab.**

3. **Change the format for Date fields to 3/1/99.**	a. On the Fields tab, **click Date.**
	b. In the Format Editor dialog box, **select the Date tab.**
	c. In the Style list box, **select 3/1/99.**

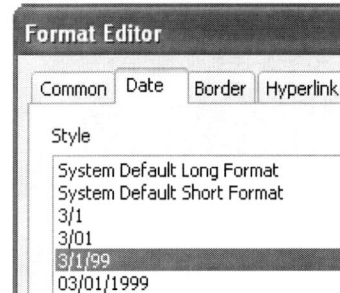

	d. **Click OK.**

4. For Group Name fields, **increase the font size.**	a. In the Options dialog box, **select the Fonts tab.**
	b. **Click Group Name Fields.**
	c. In the Size list box, **select 12.**

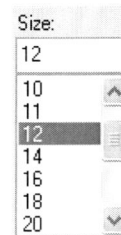

	d. To close the Font dialog box, **click OK.**

5. For all reports, **specify that section names appear abbreviated in Design view, and that they do not appear at all when you preview report data.**	a. In the Options dialog box, **select the Layout tab.**

b. In the Design View section, **check the Short Section Names check box.**

Options

Fonts	Smart T
Layout	Database

Design View
- ☑ Rulers
- ☐ Guidelines
- ☐ Grid
- ☑ Tool Tips
- ☑ Short Section Names
- ☑ Show Hidden Sections

c. In the Preview section, **uncheck the Section Names check box.**

d. To close the Options dialog box, **click OK.**

e. On the Design tab, **observe the section names.** Notice that they are now abbreviated.

f. **Position the mouse pointer over any of the abbreviated section names.** The full section name is displayed in the tooltip.

g. On the Standard toolbar, **click the Print Preview button** 🔍.

h. On the Preview tab, **observe the left side of the report.** Notice that the section names are not displayed.

i. **Save and close the report.**

TOPIC B

Specify Fields for a New Report

Once you have customized the program's default settings as needed, you are ready to create a report. In this topic, you will create a new report using fields from tables in a database file.

When you create a new report, you will need to specify which database tables and fields to include in the report. This ensures that you will be able to locate and access the specific data you need.

Database

A *database* is a collection of related data organized logically in specific categories. When creating a report in Crystal Reports, a database acts as the data source.

Relational Database

Definition:

A *relational database* is one in which data is stored in a structure of rows and columns, usually called tables, and in which data can be shared among tables through established relationships. When you build a report, you connect the database tables by connecting fields from one table to another.

Example:

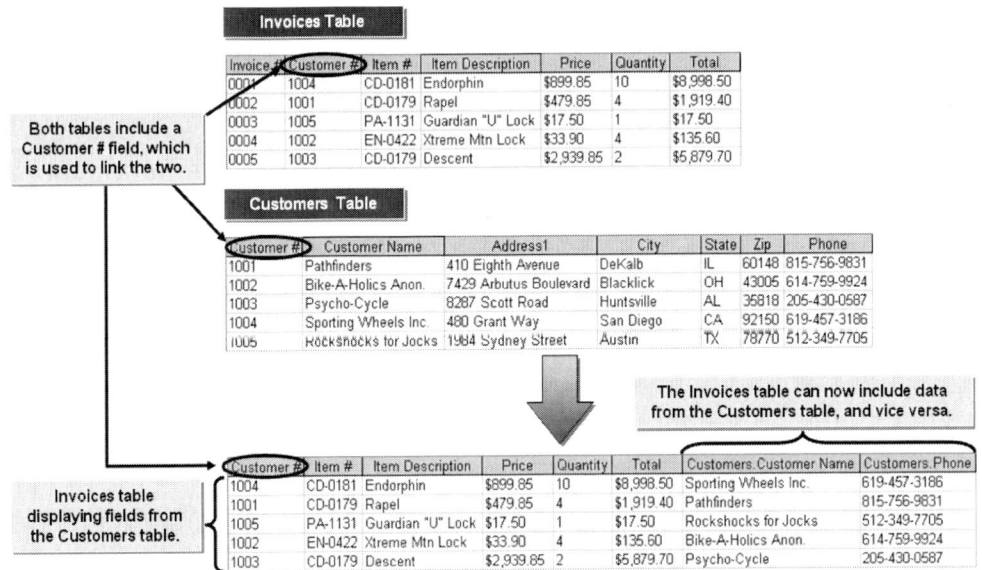

Figure 1-4: *A relational database system allows data to be shared among related database tables.*

Relational Database Links

A *link* is a common field (or fields) between two or more tables that is used to connect the tables in a relational database. The fields used to link two tables must have the same data type.

Join Types

Once a link is established between two tables, the type of join may need to be changed in an SQL/ODBC environment. Join types determine how the records from more than one table are matched. There are three common join types that you will use when linking tables. Those types are outlined in the following table.

Join Type	Function
Equal Join	Includes records from both tables only if the joining fields are equal. This is the default join in an SQL/ODBC connection.
Left Outer Join	Includes all records from the left table and records from the right table only if the joining fields are equal. This is the only type of join available when linking direct-access database tables using non-SQL drivers.
Right Outer Join	Includes all records from the right table and records from the left table only if the joining fields are equal.

Index

An *index* is a list of pointers to records in a table, sorted by value(s) in one or more fields of that table. An index is generated within the database application, sometimes automatically, and sometimes by the user. Using indexed fields in report generation within Crystal Reports speeds performance, allowing quick sorts and searches. When you are not using a native driver for the connection, fields in a primary table can be linked only to indexed fields in the related table.

The Database Expert

In Crystal Reports, you can use the Database Expert to build your reports. Using the Data tab of the Database Expert, you can browse the data source that you want to use for your report. The Links tab in the Database Expert dialog box enables you to link two or more tables.

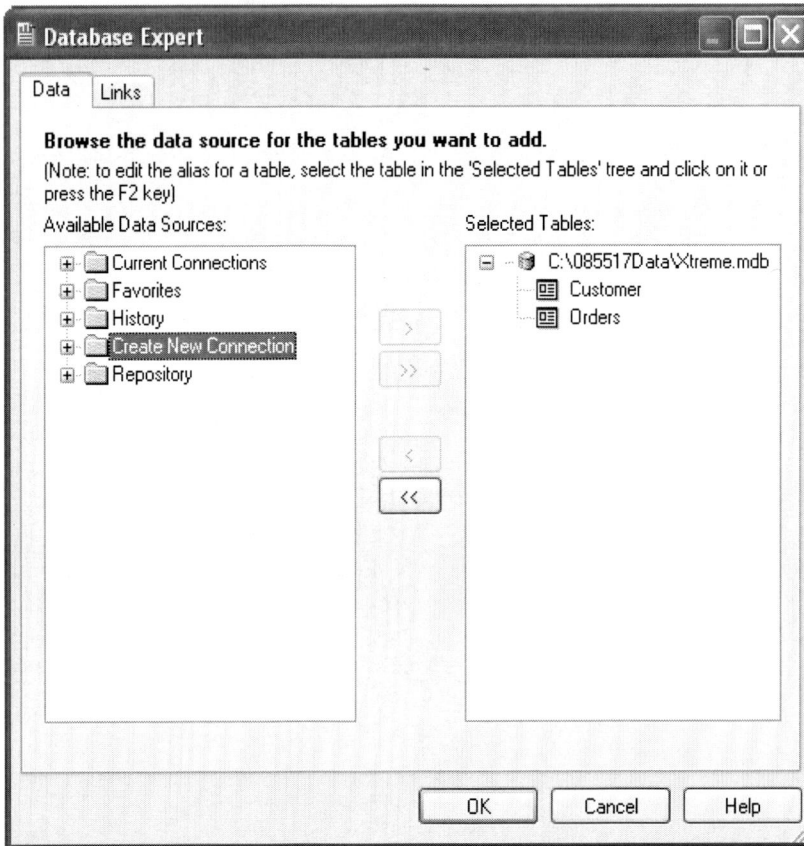

Figure 1-5: *When creating a new report, the Database Expert displays the Data tab for specifying the data source.*

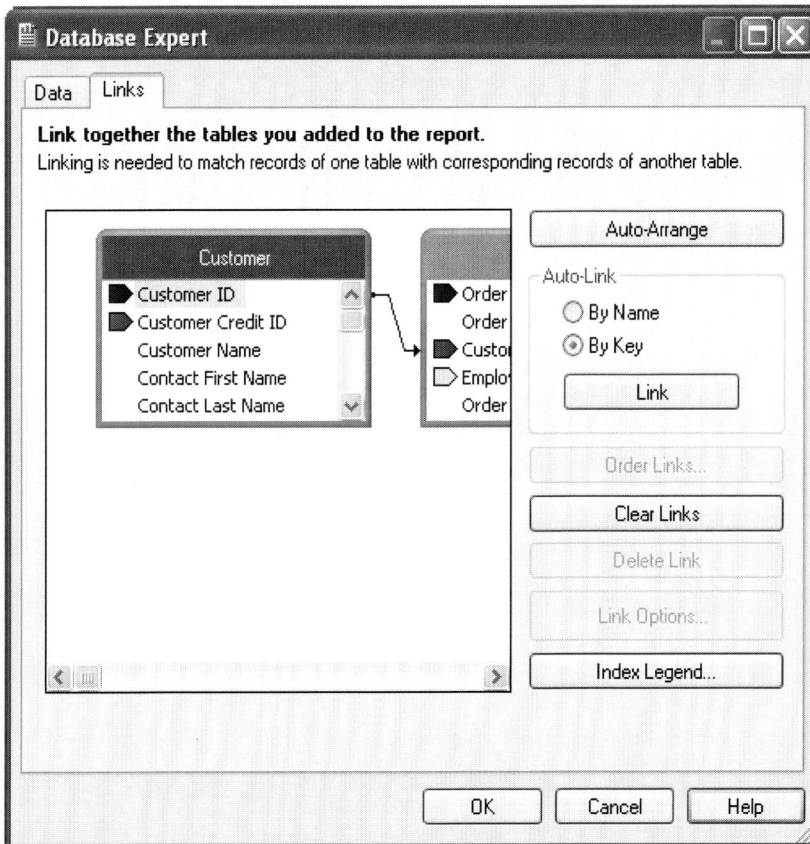

Figure 1-6: *Use the Database Expert's Links tab to link two or more tables.*

Available Data Sources

On the Data tab of the Database Expert, you can navigate through different types of folders to locate the desired data source.

Folder Type	Description
Current Connections	Displays data sources to which you are currently connected.
Favorites	Displays data sources you use often and have added to your Favorites list.
History	Displays the last five data sources you have used.
Create New Connection	Displays subfolders that include data sources to which you can connect.
Repository	Displays the contents of your repository.

The Database Expert's Links Tab

Crystal Reports will attempt to link the tables on its own. Sometimes, however, the links are not what you want, so you should always verify their accuracy.

Tab Option	Function
Links Display Area	Displays all the tables currently in your report along with any links and indexes. Note that you can scroll the Links Display area to see all tables.
Auto-Arrange	Efficiently arranges the tables within the Links display area.
Auto-Link Tables	Links the tables automatically, either by name or by key.
Clear Links	Clears the current table links.

How to Specify Fields for a New Report

Procedure Reference: Create a Report

To create a report using the Blank Report option:

There are three ways to create a report in Crystal Reports. You can create a report manually, you can create a report from an existing report, or you can use the Report Creation Wizard.

1. On the Start Page, click Blank Report.

2. In the Available Data Sources list, expand the Create New Connection folder.

3. Expand the Access/Excel (DAO) option to display the Access/Excel (DAO) dialog box.

    If you are using SQL-based databases, such as SQL Server and Oracle, you will most likely be connecting using the ODBC (RDO) or category OLE DB (ADO). Check with your database administrator.

4. In the Database Name text box, type the path and file name to indicate the desired database.

    a. To the right of the Database Name text box, click the button to display the Open dialog box.

    b. If necessary, navigate to the folder that contains the database that you want to use for your report.

    c. Select the database.

    d. Click Open to display its path in the Database Name text box.

5. Click Finish. A connection to the selected database and its contents is displayed.

6. If necessary, expand the Tables category. Select the tables you need for your report and click the Add button. The selected tables are displayed in the Selected Tables list. A Links tab is also displayed.

7. Select the Links tab. Verify that the links are correct. If they are not, link them manually. To link tables manually:

    a.   Drag the field from the first table to the field that you want to link it to in the second table. A line indicating the link will be displayed between the two tables.

    b.   Repeat the previous step until all tables are linked properly.

8.   Click OK to display the new report. If the Field Explorer is not displayed, on the Standard toolbar, click the Field Explorer button.

> 📌 You can also choose View→Field Explorer to open the Field Explorer.

9.   If necessary, expand the Database Fields category and the appropriate tables.

> 📌 In the Field Explorer, the contents of a field can be browsed by selecting the field and clicking Browse. This is helpful when faced with confusing field names. The Browse window displays the first 500 unique values for the field.

10. Add the desired fields to your report.

- Drag and drop fields.

    a.   From the Field Explorer, drag the appropriate field to the appropriate location in the report's Details section on the Design tab.

    b.   Release the mouse button.

- Place fields in a report by right-clicking.

    a.   In the Field Explorer, right-click the appropriate field and choose Insert To Report.

    b.   Place the mouse pointer in the appropriate location of the Details section and click.

- Or, place fields in a report by double-clicking.

    a.   In the Field Explorer, double-click the appropriate field.

    b.   Place the mouse pointer in the appropriate location of the Details section and click.

> 📌 In the Field Explorer, a check mark is displayed on the field icon indicating that the field has been added to the report.

> 📌 You can also edit a field label by right-clicking the field label and choosing Edit Text.

11. Save the new report to the desired location.

Standard Report Creation Wizard

When you click the New Report button on the Standard toolbar, the Standard Report Creation Wizard launches. Once you become familiar with all of the common Crystal Reports terminology and functionality, this wizard will be more helpful as it steps you through the entire report creation process.

Procedure Reference: Change Data Source Location

When creating a report, you direct Crystal Reports to wherever the data source is located so that information can be used. However, if the data source's location for a report changes, the report will not run properly until the user points the program to the new data location.

> When changing the location also involves changing the data type (that is, from ODBC to a direct-database connection), there will be no option to propagate changes. Each table location must be set individually. If the underlying database structure is different, a Map Fields dialog box will be displayed allowing you to map fields from the original source field to the new location field.

To change the location of a report's data source:

1. Open the desired report.

2. To display the Set Datasource Location dialog box, choose Database→Set Datasource Location.

3. From the Current Data Source list, select the database or table to be replaced.

4. From the Replace With list, select the new data source.

5. Click Update.

6. Repeat steps 3 through 5 as needed.

7. Close the Set Datasource Location dialog box.

8. Save and close the report.

ACTIVITY 1-2

Building the Report

Setup:
Crystal Reports is active. No reports are open.

Scenario:
You work for a company that sells bicycles and equipment. You need to create a report that summarizes customer orders stored in the Xtreme.mdb database.

What You Do	How You Do It
1. **Create a new blank report and connection to the Xtreme database.**	a. On the Start Page, under New Reports, **click Blank Report.**
	b. In the Available Data Sources list box, **expand Create New Connection.**
	c. Under Create New Connection, **expand Access/Excel (DAO).**
	d. In the Access/Excel (DAO) dialog box, to the right of the Database Name text box, **click the ellipsis button ▣ to display the Open dialog box.**
	e. If necessary, **navigate to the 085517Data folder.**
	f. In the list of files, **expand C:\085517Data\Xtreme.mdb.**

2. **Use the Customer and Orders tables in the new report.**

   a. Under Add Command, **expand Tables.**

   b. **Select Customer, press and hold down Ctrl, select Orders, and release Ctrl.**

   c. **Click the Add button** .

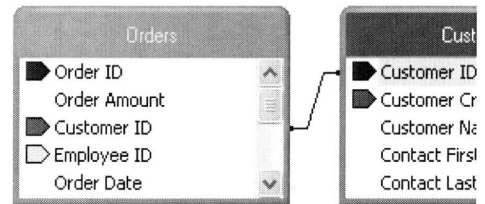

   d. **Select the Links tab.**

   e. In the Links display area, **observe the link between tables.** Notice that the Customer ID record in the Orders table is linked automatically to the Customer ID record in the Customer table.

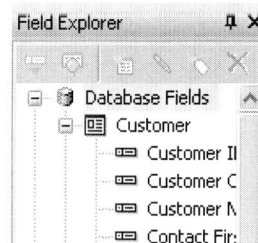

   f. **Click OK.**

---

3. **Add the customer fields.**

   ✏️ If the Field Explorer is not displayed, choose View→Field Explorer.

   a. To the right of the report, in the Field Explorer, **expand Database Fields.**

   b. To display the list of available customer fields, **expand Customer.**

c. From the Customer table, **drag the Customer ID field to the left side of the report's Details section.**

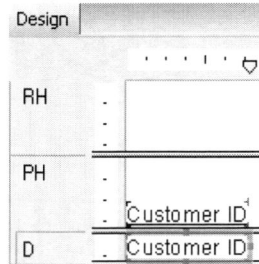

d. In the Field Explorer, a check mark is displayed on the field icon indicating that the field has been added to the report. From the Customer table, **drag the Customer Name field to the right of the Customer ID field, allowing one-eighth inch of space between fields.**

4. **Add the order fields.**

a. In the Field Explorer, **expand Orders.**

b. From the Orders table, **drag the Order ID field to the right of the Customer Name field.**

c. From the Orders table, **drag the Order Date field to the right of the Order ID field.**

d. From the Orders table, **drag the Order Amount field to the right of the Order Date field.**

5. **Save the report as *Customer Orders.rpt*.**

a. **Choose File→Save As.**

b. In the Save In drop-down list, **verify that 085517Data is displayed.**

c. In the File Name text box, to select the existing file name, **double-click it, and type *Customer Orders***

d. **Click Save.**

TOPIC C

Preview a Report

After you have created a report with the desired fields, you will be able to see field placeholders, but not the actual report data. At this point, you will typically want to view the report data itself. In this topic, you will preview a report to see the database data.

A field in a report can contain hundreds, even thousands, of data values. Until you preview a report, you will be able to see only the data placeholders. By previewing a report, you will be able to view the actual data in the fields. Also, you will know whether the fields are set up to display the data as you intended.

Navigate Using the Preview Tab

You can preview a report using the Navigation Tools toolbar on the Preview tab to move among pages.

Navigation Button	Description
Refresh	Updates report data.
Stop	Stops the reading of data from the data source.
Show First Page	Displays the first page of a report.
Show Previous Page	Moves back to the previous page of a report.
Auto Hide	Shows the page currently being displayed.
Show Next Page	Moves forward to the next page of a report.
Show Last Page	Displays the last page of a report.

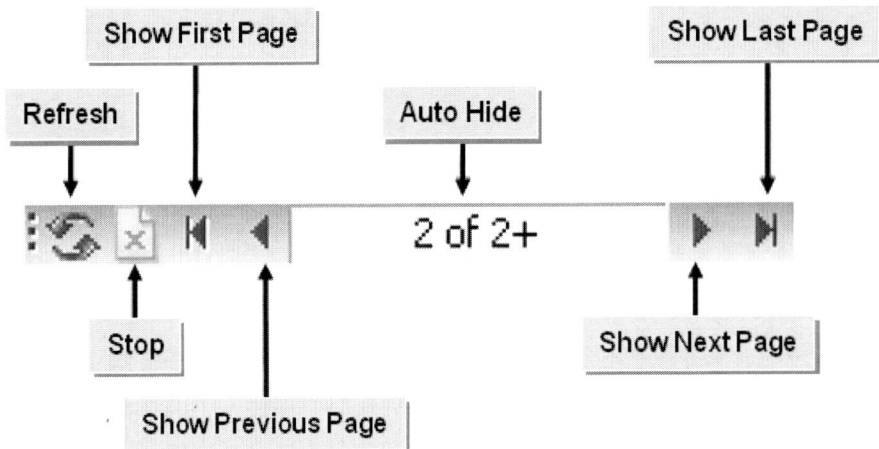

Figure 1-7: *Use the Navigation Tools toolbar to move among pages.*

The Data Age Indicator

The Data Age Indicator is displayed in the Status bar. It displays the date and time when the data was retrieved for the first time, or when it was most recently refreshed. If the data was initially refreshed or retrieved today, it displays only the time the data was retrieved or refreshed.

How to Preview a Report

Procedure Reference: Preview a Report

To preview a report:

1. On the Standard toolbar, click the Print Preview button. The report is displayed with the actual data on the Preview tab.

2. Use the navigation buttons on the Preview tab as desired to preview the report.

3. If desired, print the report.

4. If desired, close the Preview tab by clicking the tab's Close button.

HTML Preview

Not only can you see how your report will look when printed, but you can also preview how the report will appear when published to the web. Assuming your Crystal Reports installation is properly configured, clicking the HTML Preview button on the Standard toolbar, or choosing View→HTML Preview, will display a converted example of the report on an HTML Preview tab.

Preview Sample

The Preview Sample option on the View menu enables you to choose how many records you want to preview. When dealing with extremely large reports, this option can speed up your preview times significantly.

ACTIVITY 1-3

Previewing the Report

Setup:
Customer Orders.rpt is displayed on the Design tab.

Scenario:
You have added the necessary fields to your report. However, only the field placeholders are displayed in Design view. You cannot actually see the data in those fields.

What You Do	How You Do It
1. Preview the report.	a. Click the Print Preview button.

2. **On the Preview tab, what do you notice about the field placeholders?**

    a) The field placeholders remain displayed.

    b) The field placeholders display records from the database.

    c) Only a single row of database records is displayed.

    d) The field placeholders only display pound signs, #####.

3. **Navigate through the report to preview the data.**

    a. Click the Show Next Page button.

    b. **Observe the Has Been Bikes Customer Name field.** Notice that the field is not long enough to accommodate the word "consignment."

Account #	Customer Name	Order #
37	Has Been Bikes (consignmer	1,062

    c. Click the Show Last Page button.

4. **Approximately how many pages are in the report?**

    a) 2

    b) 10

    c) 25

    d) 35

5. According to the Status bar, how many records are included in the report?

    a) 253

    b) 270

    c) 1505

    d) 2191

| 6. | **Re-display the first page of the report.** | a. | Within the navigation buttons, **click the Show First Page button.** |
| | | b. | If necessary, **scroll to the top of the page.** |

TOPIC D

Modify Field Display

After initially creating a new report, you may find that some fields do not display as intended. In this topic, you will modify field labels and how fields display data.

The ability to change field labels and field formatting will allow you to control how the fields display in a report.

How to Modify Field Display

Procedure Reference: Modify Field Display

To modify the appearance of fields:

1. To change a field label, double-click the label and place the insertion point in it to edit the text as desired.

2. To modify a field's formatting, select the field, choose Format→Format Field, and make the desired changes.

    *   To customize the date and time formatting, select the Date And Time tab, and then select a format from the Style list.

    *   If you want to specify a custom date and time format, click the Customize button and specify the custom format you want.

    🔑 You can also right-click a field and choose Format Field from the shortcut menu.

ACTIVITY 1-4

Modifying Field Display

Setup:
The first page of the Customer Orders.rpt report is displayed on the Preview tab.

Scenario:
The Customer ID and Order ID fields are typically referred to as Account # and Order #, respectively. You need to modify the field labels to meet user expectations. In addition, the Order ID field currently displays both a date and a time, but you want it to display just the date, using the format 3/1/99.

What You Do	How You Do It
1. Change the Customer ID field label to *Account #*.	a. Select the Design tab.
	b. In the Page Header section, **double-click the Customer ID field label.**
	c. **Select the existing text.**
	d. **Type** *Account #*
2. Change the Order ID field label to *Order #*.	a. In the Page Header section, **double-click the Order ID field label.**
	b. **Select ID and type #**

3. Change the Order Date field to display only the date.

   a. In the Details section, **select the Order Date field.**

   b. **Choose Format→Format Field.**

   c. With the Date And Time tab selected, in the style list box, **select 3/1/99 and click OK.**

   d. To see your changes, **select the Preview tab.**

TOPIC E

Add a Report Title

Once you have previewed a report, you may decide that you want to add some type of identifier to the report that describes its contents. In this topic, you will add a title to a report.

By adding a title, anyone viewing your report will be able to immediately identify what data your report includes.

Text Objects

You can use text objects in your reports to add literal text, such as a report title or instructions on how to use the form. Text objects can also contain database fields to provide the users with access to supporting data.

How to Add a Report Title

Procedure Reference: Add a Report Title

To add a report title to the Report Header section using a text object:

1. On the Insert Tools toolbar, click the Insert Text Object button.

2. Place the insertion point anywhere in the Report Header section and click to insert a blank text object.

3. Type the title text.

4. Click outside the text object to deselect it.

5. If you want to format the title, select it and select formatting options from the Formatting toolbar.

6.   If you want to resize the field containing the title, select it and drag a sizing handle in the direction you want to resize.

🖉 If you want to resize a field and its associated field label together and select both the field and its label, then drag the left or right sizing handle as desired.

🖉 You can also resize the field on the Preview tab so that you can see the data in the field as you resize it.

ACTIVITY 1-5

Adding a Report Title

Setup:

The Customer Orders.rpt report is displayed on the Preview tab.

Scenario:

The report containing information about customer orders will eventually be viewed by others. You want those users to be able to immediately identify what is included in the report.

What You Do	How You Do It
1. On the Design tab, **add a *Customer Orders* title to the left side of the Report Header section.**	a. **Select the Design tab.**
	b. On the Insert Tools toolbar, **click the Insert Text Object button** **ab**.
	c. The mouse pointer changes to a cross hair. To insert the text object, **click in the left side of the Report Header section.**
	d. **Type *Customer Orders***

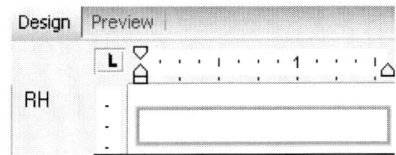

e. To deselect the text object, **click outside the text object.**

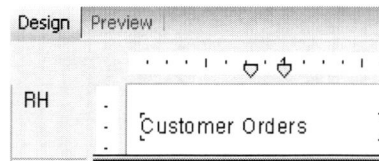

Design | Preview

RH

Customer Orders

---

2. **Format the title to 16 pt and bold it.**

a. **Select the title text object.**

b. On the Formatting toolbar, from the Font Size drop-down list, **select 16.**

c. On the Formatting toolbar, **click the Bold button** **B**.

Design | Preview

RH

Customer Orde

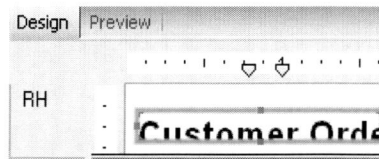

3. The title text is too big for the text object. **Resize and center the title at the top of the page.**

a. With the text object still selected, **place the mouse pointer over the right sizing handle until it is displayed as a double-headed arrow.**

b. **Drag the sizing handle to the right end of the ruler.**

c. On the Formatting toolbar, **click the Align Center button** ☰.

d. To increase the field's height, **place the mouse pointer over the text object's bottom-center sizing handle and drag down.**

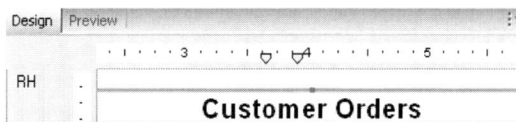

Design | Preview

RH

Customer Orders

e. To deselect the title, **click in a blank area of the report.**

TOPIC F

Position Fields

As you design a report, you will often want to arrange the fields to further organize the report. In this topic, you will reposition fields to achieve more equal spacing between fields.

The fields in a report may not fit correctly or the spacing may not look right. By balancing the positioning of fields, the report will be easier to read and will look better.

Guidelines

Guidelines appear as small triangles within the horizontal ruler. Each field has a corresponding guideline on the ruler that represents the field's position. By default, a guideline corresponds to a field's alignment. A red indicator appears on each field or other object, indicating the position at which it is attached to its corresponding guideline.

> You can also add guidelines to the vertical ruler. To do so, simply click in the white area of the vertical ruler.

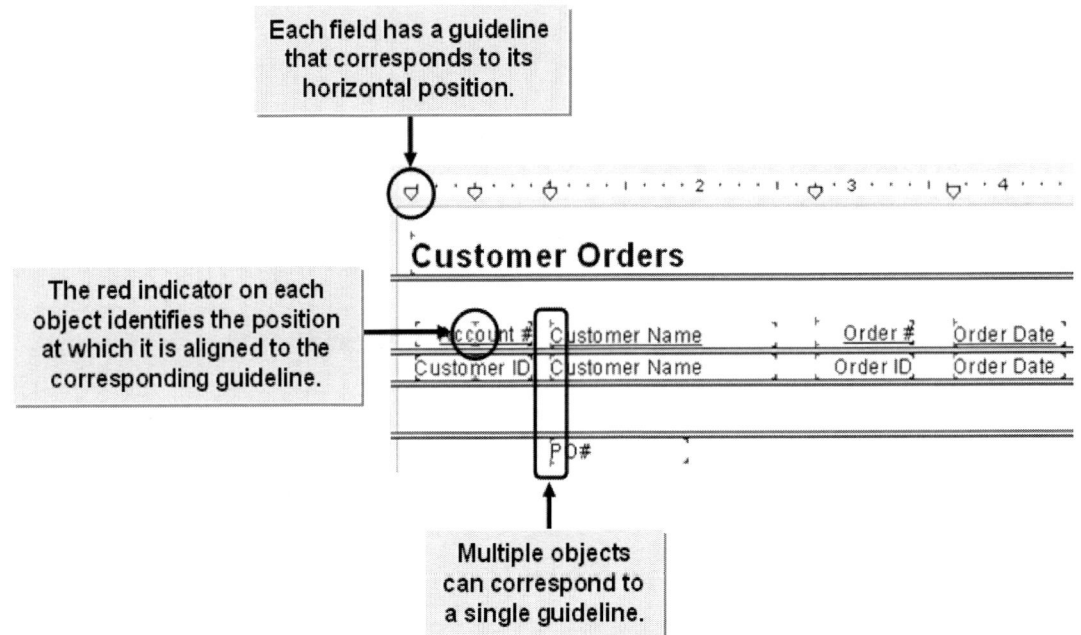

Figure 1-8: *Guidelines correspond to each field's position.*

How to Position Fields

Procedure Reference: Position Fields in a Report

To position fields using guidelines:

✐ After placing a field in a report, guideline arrows display on the ruler at the left edge of string and date fields. Guideline arrows for number fields run along the right edge of the field.

1. On the Design tab, if necessary, resize the object you want to move by positioning the mouse pointer on the right or left sizing handle and dragging. (Resizing a field will also resize its corresponding field label.)

2. On the ruler, locate the guideline that is associated with the object you want to move.

3. Drag the field's guideline to the desired location.

4. Preview the report to verify that the field's position is correct.

Procedure Reference: Use Guidelines

To use guidelines:

1. Perform any of the following actions.

    *   To add a guideline for an object that does not have one, click in the ruler to add the guideline.

    *   To associate a guideline with an object, drag the object so that it aligns as desired to the guideline. Alternatively, you could drag the guideline to align to the object.

    *   To align to a different part of the guideline, drag the field horizontally so that it aligns to the guideline's left, center, or right edge.

        ✐ To vertically or horizontally align report elements without using guidelines, you can select multiple fields and align them using the Format→Align submenu.

    *   To remove a guideline, drag it away from the ruler.

ACTIVITY 1-6

Positioning Fields

Setup:
The Customer Orders.rpt report is displayed on the Design tab.

Scenario:
Now that you have added the title, you look at the fields and realize that some of them need to be resized and moved to improve the report's appearance.

What You Do	How You Do It
1. On the Design tab, **adjust the Customer Name field's position.**	a. **Place the mouse pointer over the guideline for the Customer Name field.**

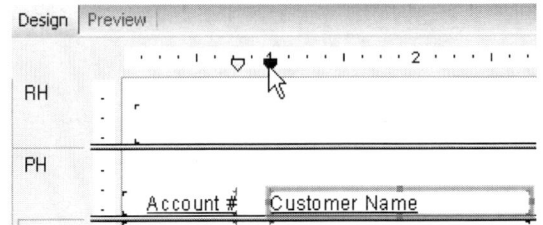

📌 If the guide for the customer name is missing, you didn't leave enough space between the fields when you added the Customer Name field from the Customer table. Delete the field and re-add it, leaving one-eighth inch between them.

	b. **Drag the Customer Name guideline to the 1.5″ mark on the horizontal ruler.**

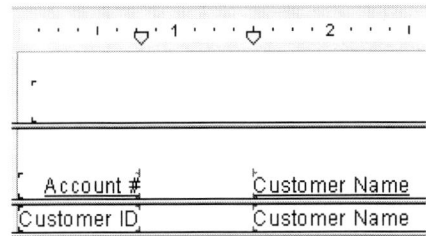

2. **Move the Account # field to the right.**	a. **Place the mouse pointer over the guideline for the Account # field.**
	b. **Drag the Account # guideline to the 1″ mark on the ruler.**

3. **Move the Order Amount field, the Order Date field, and the Order # field.**

    a. Using the associated guideline, **move the Order Amount field to 7.5".**

    b. Using the associated guideline, **move the Order Date field to 5".**

    c. Using the associated guideline, **move the Order # field to 4.5".**

    > The locations of the fields do not have to be exact.

4. **Resize the Customer Name field.**

    a. In the Details section, **select the Customer Name field.**

    b. **Place the mouse pointer over the right sizing handle and drag it to the right to 3.75".**

5. **Preview the report.**

    a. **Select the Preview tab.**

    b. **Navigate to the second page of the report.**

    c. **Observe the Has Been Bikes Customer Name field.** Notice that all field data is now displayed.

    Customer Name
    Has Been Bikes (consignment)

TOPIC G

Add Fields from Other Tables

After creating a report, you may find that it does not contain all the fields necessary, so you may need to add new tables to access the fields you want to display. In this topic, you will add fields to a report from an additional table.

Adding tables to your report will give you the ability to access additional fields so you can display the desired data in the report.

How to Add Fields from Other Tables

Procedure Reference: Add Fields from Other Tables

To add fields from other tables to an existing report:

1. Display the Database Expert dialog box.
   - Choose Database→Database Expert.
   - Or, on the Expert Tools toolbar, click the Database Expert button.

2. Use the Available Data Sources section to locate the desired database, creating a new connection if necessary. Then, double-click the desired table(s) to add them.

   You can also click the Add button to add a selected table.

3. On the Links tab, confirm that the links are correct, modifying them as needed, and click OK.

4. In the Field Explorer, expand the new table and drag the desired fields to the report.

Procedure Reference: Remove a Table

To remove a table from a report:

1. Choose Database→Database Expert.

2. In the Selected Tables section, select the table to be removed.

3. Click the Remove button.

4. Repeat steps 2 and 3 for any additional tables you need to remove and click OK.

ACTIVITY 1-7

Adding Fields from Additional Tables

Setup:
The second page of the Customer Orders.rpt report is displayed on the Preview tab.

Scenario:
In Customer Orders.rpt, you need to display the unit price for the product ordered, along with the quantity ordered for each record. That information is located in the Orders_Detail table.

What You Do	How You Do It
1. Add the Orders_Detail table to the report.	a. Choose Database→Database Expert.
	b. In the Available Data Sources list box, **double-click Orders Detail.**
	Selected Tables: □ ─ 🗄 C:\085517Data\Xtreme.mdb 　　🎞 Customer 　　🎞 Orders 　　🎞 Orders_Detail
	c. To display the Links tab, **click OK.**
	d. The Orders_Detail table is linked to the Orders table. **Click OK.**
	e. To refresh the data, **click OK.**
2. To make room for the new fields, **reposition the existing fields.**	a. On the Preview tab, **shorten the Order Date field.**
	◇ · · · 6 · · ┊ · · · 7 · · · ◇ Order Date ┊ Order Amount 12/12/03 ↔ $65.70
	b. **Select the Design tab.**
	c. **Use the guideline to drag the Order Date field to the left.**

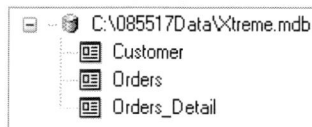

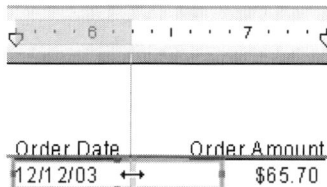

d. **Drag the Order Amount field to the far right of the report.**

```
· 4 · · ·  ⇩ ⇩ · 5 · · · · I · · · 6 · · · I · · · 7 · · · I · · ·ᴄ
```

ner Orders

Order #	Order Date		Order Amount
Order ID	Order Date		Order Amount

3. **Place the Unit Price and Quantity fields to the right side of the report.**

a. In the Field Explorer, **scroll down and expand the Orders_Detail table.**

b. In the Details section, to the right of the Order Date field, **drag the Unit Price field.**

c. In the Details section, to the right of the Unit Price field, **drag the Quantity field.**

```
· 4 · · · ⇩ ⇩ · 5 · · · · I · · · 6 · ⇩ · I · · · 7 · · · I · · ·ᴄ
```

ner Orders

Order #	Order Date	Unit Price	Quantity	Order Amount
Order ID	Order Date	Unit Price	Quantity	Order Amount

d. **Select the Preview tab.**

e. **Observe the two new fields.** Notice that the Unit Price multiplied by the Quantity may equal the Order Amount. If an order consists of several units, each will represent a portion of the total Order Amount.

f. **Adjust the field positions as necessary.**

g. **Save and close the report.**

Lesson 1 Follow-up

In this lesson, you created a report from information stored in an existing database. You modified default report settings so that the report would be displayed as desired. Then, you built the report by adding a report title, aligning fields, and previewing the data. Now, when you need to display specific information from a database, you will be prepared to provide that detail in a report.

1. What default settings do you plan to change in the reports you create?

2. Considering the databases you use on the job, what types of data will your reports include?

NOTES

LESSON 2

Displaying Specific Report Data

Lesson Objectives:

In this lesson, you will use a report to present specific data in the desired order.

You will:

- Find data in a report.
- Sort data in a report.
- Filter data in a report.

Introduction

Reports may include large amounts of data. At times, you will want to reference only portions of that data. Therefore, you need to find ways to quickly access specific data in the report. In this lesson, you will use options for displaying specific report data.

There is nothing more frustrating than having access to data but not being able to quickly find the details you want. Crystal Reports provides you with the means necessary to locate that information.

TOPIC A

Find Data

When you are previewing a report, you might need to quickly locate one record in the report. In this topic, you will use the Find dialog box to locate a specific record.

You have a report that contains thousands of customer records. A customer just called and you need to find the record for that customer. Looking through the report for that specific record could take quite a bit of time. Using the Find dialog box, you can quickly locate the record you need.

How to Find Data

Procedure Reference: Find Data in a Report

To locate data in an open report:

1. If necessary, display the Preview tab, as the search capability is only available on this tab.

2. Display the Find dialog box.
    *   On the Standard toolbar, click the Find button.
    *   Choose Edit→Find.
    *   Or, press Ctrl+F.

3. In the Find What text box, type the information you want to find.

    Make sure that your search strings match the field formatting. When searching for number fields, if data is formatted to show the thousands separator, the separator must be used in the Find What text box. The same is not true for decimal formatting. Numbers will be found regardless of the decimal format.

    ✍ When formatting might return unexpected results, users are advised to use the Advanced Find option, which allows users to select a specific field for searching. Search results are not impacted by formatting when using this option.

4. If desired, specify whether or not to use Match Case, Match Whole Word Only, and Direction options.

5. Click Find Next to locate the specified record. If there are multiple instances of the search term, clicking Find Next will display the next instance. If no other instances are found, Crystal Reports will notify you that it has finished searching the document.

6. Click Cancel to close the Find dialog box.

Search Expert

The Find dialog box is very basic and is fine for performing common searches. However, if you need more complex functionality, click the Advanced Find button to display the Search Expert. The expert allows you to choose specific fields, add search conditions, and modify the search formula manually.

ACTIVITY 2-1

Finding Data

Data Files:

- Specific Orders.rpt

Setup:

No files are open in Crystal Reports. The Start Page is displayed.

Scenario:

You received a call regarding a problem with Order # 2,783 and Order # 1,092. The customers apparently sent checks for the incorrect amounts. You need to quickly locate the records so you can identify the correct amounts.

What You Do	How You Do It
1. Open the Specific Orders.rpt report.	a. On the Standard toolbar, **click the Open button** [icon].
	b. The contents of the folder C:\085517Data are displayed in the Open dialog box. **Select Specific Orders.rpt and click Open.**
	c. **Click Open.**
	d. **Verify that the Preview tab is selected.**

2. **Locate Order # 2,783.**

   a. On the Standard toolbar, **click the Find button** 🔍.

   b. In the Find What text box, **type *2,783***

   c. **Click Find Next.**

   d. To close the Find dialog box, **click Cancel.**

   e. If necessary, to display the record's Order Amount, **scroll to the right.**

---

3. **What is the correct amount for Mad Mountain Bikes' Order # 2,783?**

   a) $1,781.25

   b) $67.80

   c) $1,439.55

   d) $15.50

---

4. **Locate Order # 1,092.**

   a. **Click the Find button** 🔍.

   b. In the Find What text box, **type *1,092***

   c. **Click Find Next.**

---

5. **What happened when you clicked Find Next?**

   a) The string was found.

   b) The string was not found.

   c) Multiple records were found.

   d) The Search Expert was displayed.

---

6. The record must be before Order # 2,783. **Search backward for Order # 1,092.**

   a. To close the warning dialog box, **click OK.**

   b. In the Find dialog box, under Direction, **select Up.**

   c. **Click Find Next.**

   d. To close the Find dialog box, **click Cancel.**

---

7. What is the correct amount for City Cyclists' Order # 1,092?

    a) $42.00

    b) $62.33

    c) $3,884.25

    d) $6,682.98

TOPIC B

Sort Data

By using the Find dialog box, you quickly found a specific record in a report. The order in which data is displayed in a report can also help you find data quickly. In this topic, you will organize the data in a report by sorting.

Just as words in a dictionary are organized alphabetically, you can organize the records in a report based on criteria you specify, making the report easier to read and the data easier to interpret.

Data Sort Order

When you use database data in a report, the records are displayed in the order they were entered into the database. That order is called the *natural order*. You can sort the data in *ascending order*, so that the records are sorted from smallest to largest (that is, 1 to 9, A to Z). You can also choose *descending order*, so the records are sorted from largest to smallest (that is, 9 to 1, Z to A).

How to Sort Data

Procedure Reference: Sort Data

To sort the records in a report:

1. Display the Record Sort Expert.

    • On the Expert Tools toolbar, click the Record Sort Expert button.

    • Or, choose Report→Record Sort Expert.

2. Add and remove fields from the Sort Fields list.

    • To add a field to the Available Fields list, double-click the desired field.

        To add a field to the Sort Fields list, you can select the field and click the Add button. To remove a field from the Sort Fields list, click the Remove button.

    • To sort the records secondarily by another field value, add the other field to the Available Fields list below the first field.

    • To remove a field from the Sort Fields list, double-click the field you want to remove.

- To re-position the field sort order in the Sort Fields list, select the field you want to move, then, above the list, click the Up or Down button.

3. If desired, in the Sort Direction box, select the direction by which you want to sort. Ascending is the default sort order.

4. Click OK to sort the report.

ACTIVITY 2-2

Sorting Data

Setup:
The first page of the Specific Orders.rpt report is displayed on the Preview tab.

Scenario:
The Specific Orders report tracks customer orders. You need to know which customers have placed the largest orders in terms of dollar amounts, and then you want to identify the most recent order for Alley Cat Cycles.

What You Do	How You Do It
1. Sort the report by the Order Amount field.	a. On the Expert Tools toolbar, **click the Record Sort Expert button** [icon]. b. In the Available Fields list box, **double-click the Orders.Order Amount field.** 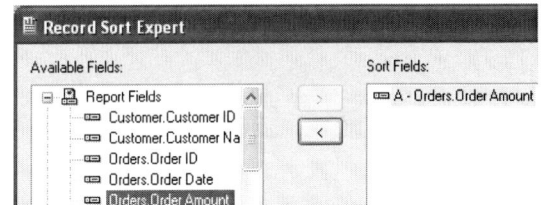 c. In the Sort Direction box, **select the Descending option.** d. **Click OK.**

2. Which company placed the largest order?

   a) Bikes for Tykes

   b) The Great Bike Shop

   c) Insane Cycle

   d) Wheels and Stuff

3.	Remove the Order Amount sort.	a. Display the Record Sort Expert dialog box.
		b. In the Sort Fields list box, **select Orders.Order Amount.**
		c. **Click the Remove button** ⟨ **.**

4.	Sort the report by Customer Name, and secondarily by Order Date.	a. To the Sort Fields list box, **add the Customer.Customer Name field.**
		b. To the Sort Fields list, **add the Orders.Order Date field.**
		c. **Select the Descending option.**
		d. **Click OK.**

5. What was the date of the most recent order for Alley Cat Cycles?

    a) 5/26/04

    b) 6/21/04

    c) 4/9/05

    d) 3/7/05

TOPIC C

Filter Data by a Single Criterion

Another way to locate specific report data is to filter the data so that only data that meets specific criteria is visible. In this topic, you will filter data based on the contents of a particular field.

By filtering data in a report, you will display only the records that you need, making the report easier to read and quicker to access because less information is displayed.

Filter

If you do not want all the records to display in a report, you can filter the report. A *filter* allows you to display certain records based on specific criteria. *Criteria* are the rules on which a decision is based.

Comparison Operators

Definition:

A *comparison operator* is a statement you can use to compare data in a field that has a fixed value with the content of another field.

📌 A comparison operator can compare any values of the same data type, including database fields, constant values, parameters, and formula values, just to name a few.

📌 For more information on comparison operators, choose Help→Crystal Reports Help and search for comparison operators.

Example:

Here are some examples of comparison operators and their symbols.

Comparison Operator	Symbol
Is equal to	=
Not equal to	<>
Is less than	<
Is greater than	>

How to Filter Data by a Single Criterion

Procedure Reference: Filter Data Using a Single Criterion

To filter data using a single criterion:

1. Select the desired report field in which to filter.

   📌 If you do not select a field first, then when you click the Select Expert button, the Choose Field dialog box will be displayed. From there, you can select the desired field in which to filter and click OK to display the Select Expert dialog box.

   📌 You can filter data from the Design or Preview tab.

2. Display the Select Expert dialog box.
   - On the Expert Tools toolbar, click the Select Expert button.
   - Choose Report→Select Expert.
   - Or, right-click and choose Select Expert.

3. From the first drop-down list, select the appropriate comparison operator, or click Show Formula and type one in the text box.

4. In the second drop-down list, type or select a value.

   📌 If you are on the Preview tab when you modify selection criteria, as soon as you close out of the Select Expert, you will be asked whether you want to use saved data or refresh the data.

5. Click OK to filter the data.

6. If desired, refresh the data.

Procedure Reference: Delete a Filter

To remove a filter:

1. Display the Select Expert dialog box.

2. If necessary, display the appropriate field tab.

3. Click Delete to remove the filter and click OK.

4. If desired, refresh the data.

ACTIVITY 2-3

Filtering Data by a Single Criterion

Setup:

The first page of the Specific Orders.rpt report is displayed on the Preview tab.

Scenario:

The marketing department plans to send out coupons to all customers who have placed individual orders for more than $500. Additionally, marketing wants a list of all customers who have placed individual orders of $5,000 or more, so they can be enrolled in the new Platinum Club.

What You Do	How You Do It
1. Display the Select Expert dialog box for the Orders.Order Amount field.	a. Select the Design tab.
	b. Select the Order Amount field.
	![Order # / Order Date / Order Amount table with Order ID / Order Date / Order Amount row]
	c. On the Expert Tools toolbar, **click the Select Expert button** ![icon].
2. Display only those records with an order amount greater than $500.	a. In the Select Expert dialog box, on the Orders.Order Amount tab, from the drop-down list, **select Is Greater Than.**

b. In the second text box, **type *500***

Select Expert	
Orders.Order Amount	<New>
is greater than ▾	500

c. **Click OK.**

d. **Select the Preview tab.**

Change In Record Selection Formula
? Use saved data from: 4/20/2005 9:31 ?
Use Saved Data   Refresh Data

e. A message dialog box is displayed. **Click Refresh Data.**

---

3. **According to the Status bar, how many orders were placed for more than $500?**

   a) 1,307

   b) 1,281

   c) 100

   d) 2,191

---

4. **Display only those records with an order amount greater than or equal to $5,000.**

   a. With the Order Amount field still selected, **click the Select Expert button** 📇.

   b. On the Orders.Order Amount tab, from the first drop-down list, **select Is Greater Than Or Equal To.**

   c. In the second drop-down list, **type *5000***

   d. **Click OK.**

   e. **Click Refresh Data.**

---

5. **According to the Status bar, how many orders were placed for more than $5,000?**

   a) 296

   b) 1,320

   c) 2,735

   d) 0

---

6. Remove the filter to re-display all records.

   a. Click the Select Expert button.

   b. On the Orders.Order Amount tab, **click Delete.**

   c. **Click OK and click Refresh Data.**

7. Save and close the report.

Lesson 2 Follow-up

In this lesson, you used options for displaying specific report data. Once you located the desired data, you sorted and filtered it so that it was displayed exactly as you wanted. Being able to find and display details exactly as you want them will make your reports much more efficient for everyone.

1. How often will you sort and filter data in your reports?

2. Considering the types of data you typically report on, what types of filters might you create?

NOTES

LESSON 3
Grouping Report Data

Lesson Time
2 hour(s) to 2 hour(s), 30 minutes

Lesson Objectives:

In this lesson, you will create groups to summarize report data.

You will:

- Insert a group in a report.
- Add summaries to a report.
- Format fields and labels for summary information.
- Change the display of grouped data.
- Add a second-level grouping.
- Filter group data.
- Create a Top N sort group.

Introduction

You can now display report data the way you want. To continue organizing a report is to group and, if desired, summarize the data in each group. In this lesson, you will group and summarize data in a report.

By grouping and summarizing similar data, your reports will be better organized and the information will be more meaningful to your audience.

TOPIC A

Insert a Group

Before you can summarize data in a report, you should group similar data. In this topic, you will insert a group in a report.

By grouping your data, you will be able to show associated information together, creating a better organized report that is easier to understand. You can easily navigate in a long report when it is grouped.

Groups

Definition:

A *group* is a collection of related data based on a selected field or formula that displays in a desired order. When you create a group, a Group Header section and a Group Footer section are displayed. The Group Header section can contain a Group Name field. You can use the Group Header or Group Footer section to display summary information for the group.

- Customers living in the same region.
- Orders placed by the same customer.
- Orders sold by the same sales representative.

Removal of a Group Name field from a report will not impact the report grouping.

Example:

Some examples of groups include:
- Customers living in the same region.
- Orders placed by the same customer.
- Orders sold by the same sales representative.

A Group Header section is created to display the Company Name field above each group.

These report records are grouped by the Company Name field.

22	Crank Components	1,659	05/29/04	$10,605.18
22	Crank Components	1,402	03/04/04	$515.67
22	Crank Components	1,718	06/15/04	$15,492.32
22	Crank Components	1,458	03/28/04	$659.70
12	Hooked on Helmets	2,219	10/14/04	$2,678.87
12	Hooked on Helmets	1,276	02/08/04	$3,815.34
12	Hooked on Helmets	1,654	05/26/04	$8,819.55
12	Hooked on Helmets	1,824	07/04/04	$4,053.45
4	Psycho-Cycle	2,231	10/18/04	$8,819.55
4	Psycho-Cycle	1,398	03/02/04	$3,147.21
4	Psycho-Cycle	1,337	02/22/03	$1,067.50
4	Psycho-Cycle	2,414	11/23/04	$6,113.10

Figure 3-1: *Grouping records organizes them by the field you specify.*

Group Tree View

When you create a group, the Group Tree view is displayed. The Group Tree view creates a split screen, with the Group Tree displayed in the left pane, showing a high-level outline of the report. In the right pane, the contents of the report are displayed. You can use the Group Tree view to quickly move to a particular group by selecting the node for that group.

Clicking a group name in the Group Tree pane displays the corresponding group's contents in the right pane.

Figure 3-2: *The Group Tree displays an outline of the report in the left pane.*

How to Insert a Group

Procedure Reference: Insert a Group

To insert a group in a report:

1. With the Design tab displayed, open the Insert Group dialog box.

    • On the Insert Tools toolbar, click the Insert Group button.

    • Or, choose Insert→Group.

    🖈 You can also create a group by choosing Report→Group Expert.

2. On the Common tab, from the first drop-down list, select the field by which you want to group the data.

3. From the second drop-down list, select the order by which you want to sort the group and click OK.

4. If necessary, display the Group Tree.

- On the Standard toolbar, click the Toggle Group Tree button.

- Or, choose View→Group Tree.

5. If the Group Tree pane is too narrow, preventing the full group names from being displayed, place the mouse pointer over the desired item to display its full name in a tooltip.

You can widen the Group Tree pane by dragging the pane's right edge.

6. If desired, preview the report and click a group name to display the group data.

ACTIVITY 3-1

Inserting a Group

Data Files:

- Customer Grouping.rpt

Setup:

No files are open in Crystal Reports. The Start Page is displayed.

Scenario:

You created the Customer Grouping.rpt report, which contains customer order data. However, it isn't easy to review all of a customer's orders because there's no easy way to navigate from customer to customer.

What You Do	How You Do It
1. Create a group by Customer Name in ascending order.	a. Open the Customer Grouping.rpt report.
	b. Observe the Group Tree. Notice that the report currently does not contain any groups.
	Design Preview ✕
	Customer Group
	c. Select the Design tab.
	d. On the Insert Tools toolbar, **click the Insert Group button** 📇.

e. On the Common tab, from the top drop-down list, **select Customer.Customer Name.**

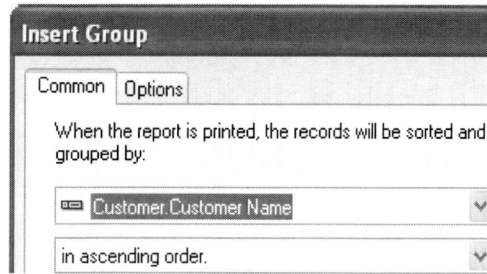

f. With In Ascending Order displayed in the second drop-down list, **click OK.**

g. **Observe the report.** Notice that a new Group Header #1 section, with a Group #1 Name object, and a Group Footer #1 section now surround the Details section.

---

2. **Preview the data for the customer, Spokes For Folks.**

a. **Select the Preview tab.**

b. **Observe the Group Tree.** Notice that the report now contains a group for each customer.

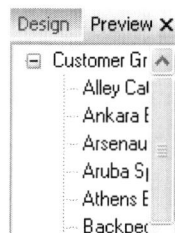

c. In the Group Tree, **scroll down until the customers that begin with "S" are displayed.**

d. Using the tooltip as a guide, **locate Spokes For Folks.**

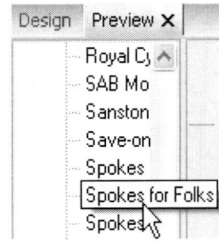

e. To display the customer's data, **click Spokes For Folks.**

⚠ To display the data for Spokes For Folks, you may need to click the Show Next Page button if the data are split over two pages.

TOPIC B

Add Summaries

After you have added a group to a report, you can summarize the grouped data. In this topic, you will add summaries to a grouped report.

By adding summaries to your report, you can mathematically summarize the data by group rather than for all records in the report.

Summary Operations

A *summary operation* is a type of mathematical function that you can use to summarize the data in a report.

Summary Operation	Description
Sum	Adds the values for the selected field.
Average	Calculates the average for the selected field.

Summary Operation	Description
Minimum	Calculates the lowest value for the selected field.
Maximum	Calculates the highest value for the selected field.
Count	Calculates the total number of records for the selected field.

How to Add Summaries

Procedure Reference: Add Summaries

To add group and grand summaries to a report:

1. On the Design tab, in the Details section, select the field that you want to summarize.

2. Display the Insert Summary dialog box.
   - On the Insert Tools toolbar, click the Insert Summary button.
   - Choose Insert→Summary.
   - Or, right-click the desired field and choose Insert→Summary.

3. From the Calculate This Summary drop-down list, select the desired summary operation.

4. From the Summary Location drop-down list, select a summary type.
   - Add the summary to the desired group by selecting that group.
   - Or, add a grand total summary by selecting Grand Total (Report Footer).

5. Click OK to insert the summaries.

ACTIVITY 3-2

Adding Totals

Setup:

The Customer Grouping.rpt report is open and the Spokes For Folks group is displayed on the Preview tab.

Scenario:

After grouping the report, you need to display the sum of the order amounts for each customer, and a grand total for the whole report.

What You Do	How You Do It
1. Create a summary for each customer's order amounts.	a. Select the Design tab.
	b. In the Details section, **select the Order Amount field.**
	c. On the Insert Tools toolbar, **click the Insert Summary button Σ.**
	d. In the Calculate This Summary drop-down list, **verify that Sum is displayed.**
	e. From the Summary Location drop-down list, **select Group #1: Customer.Customer Name - A.**

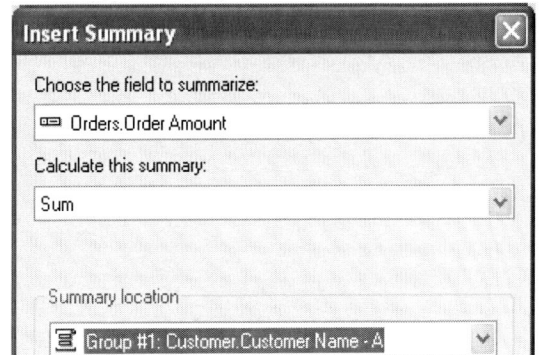

	f. **Click OK.**
	g. **Observe the Group Footer #1 section.** Notice that the summary was added.

2. Create a report grand total for the Order Amount field.

   a. Select the Order Amount field.

   b. Click the Insert Summary button.

   c. Verify that the Summary Location drop-down list displays Grand Total (Report Footer).

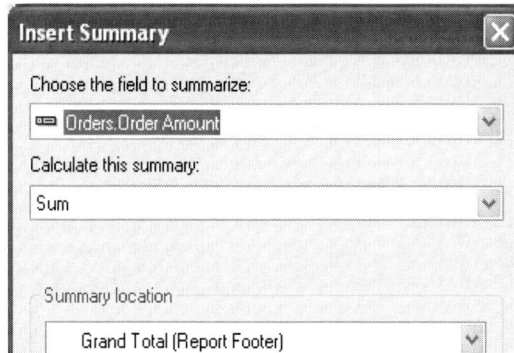

Insert Summary

Choose the field to summarize:

  Orders.Order Amount

Calculate this summary:

  Sum

Summary location

  Grand Total (Report Footer)

   d. Click OK.

   e. Observe the Report Footer section. Notice that the grand total summary was added.

---

3. Preview the order amount summary for Bikes For Tykes.

   a. Select the Preview tab.

   b. In the Group Tree, click Bikes For Tykes.

---

4. What is the order amount summary total for Bikes For Tykes?

   a) $48,086.23

   b) $35,376.01

   c) $47,225.53

   d) $959.70

---

5. Preview the grand total order amount summary for all customers.

   a. In the report's navigation buttons, click the Show Last Page button.

   b. The grand total is too large to be displayed by the Summary field. Select the Summary field.

   c. Drag the field's left sizing handle to the 5.75″ mark.

---

6. What is the grand total for all customers?

    a) $50,512.26

    b) $989.55

    c) $2,939.85

    d) $3,982,734.36

TOPIC C

Format Summary Information

After summarizing data, you may want to draw attention to it. In this topic, you will format summary information.

If a report includes subtotal and grand total information, you may want to format the totals to make them easier to recognize at a glance.

How to Format Summary Information

Procedure Reference: Format Summary Information

To format summary data so that it stands out from the surrounding data:

1. If necessary, to change the type color for a field or field label:

    a. Select the object.

    b. On the Formatting toolbar, from the Font Color drop-down list, select a color.

2. If necessary, to add a border to a field or field label:

    a. Select the appropriate object.

    b. On the Formatting toolbar, from the Borders drop-down list, select the desired border.

3. If necessary, to create a new label with the same formatting as an existing label:

    a. Hold down Ctrl and drag a copy of the existing label to a new location.

    b. In the label copy, modify the text as needed.

4. To format a label to match an existing label:

    a. Select the label with the formatting you want to copy.

    b. On the Standard toolbar, click the Format Painter button.

    c. Click the label you want to format to paste the copied formatting without affecting the data.

> You can also right-click an object whose formatting you want to copy, choose Format Painter from the shortcut menu, then click another object to which you want to apply the formatting.

ACTIVITY 3-3

Formatting Summary Data

Setup:

The grand total for the Customer Grouping.rpt report is displayed on the Preview tab.

Scenario:

After previewing the summary data, you are concerned that it may not be easy for a reader to distinguish the totals and grand total from the other numbers in the report.

What You Do	How You Do It
1. Add a field label for the group summary field, and format both the field and label.	a. Select the Design tab.
	b. In the Group Footer #1 section, **insert a text object at the 5″ mark.**
	c. Type *Group Total* and deselect the label.

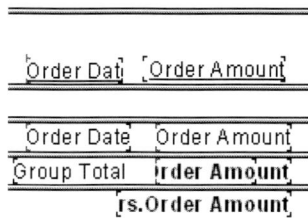

	d. **Select the Group Total label and bold it.**
	e. To decrease the Group Total label's width, **drag the label's right sizing handle left to the 6″ mark.**
	f. With the Group Total label still selected, **press and hold down Ctrl and click the adjacent Order Amount group summary field.**

g. On the Formatting toolbar, from the Font Color drop-down list, **select the Navy swatch.**

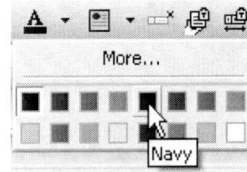

h. In the Group Footer #1 section, at approximately the 4.25" mark, **click the blank area to deselect the objects.**

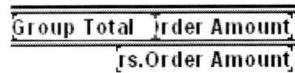

---

2. **Add a field label for the grand total.**

a. While holding down Ctrl, drag a copy of the Group Total label down into the Report Footer section, so the label's left edge is at the 4.75" mark.

b. **Double-click the new label and select the word "Group."**

c. **Type** *Grand* **and deselect the label.**

---

3. **Format the Order Amount field in the Report Footer to match the Order Amount field in the Group Footer.**

a. In the Group Footer #1 section, **click the Order Amount field.**

b. On the Standard toolbar, **click the Format Painter button** 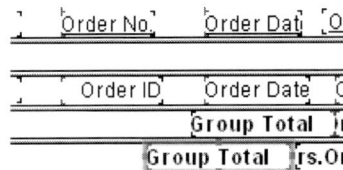.

c. To apply the copied formatting, in the Report Footer, **click the Order Amount field.**

---

4. **Preview the report.**

a. **Select the Preview tab.**

b. **Observe the grand total information at the end of the report.** Notice that the grand total and the group's summary total are identically formatted.

5. You need to make the grand total information stand out more prominently from the surrounding data. **Format the Grand Total field and field label to appear as 12-pt text with a horizontal line above them.**

a. **Select the Design tab.**

b. In the Report Footer, **while holding down Ctrl, select both grand total objects.**

c. **Move both objects to the bottom of the Report Footer section.**

Order No.   Order Date   Order Amount

Order ID   Order Date   Order Amount
Group Total   rder Amount

Grand Total   rs.Order Amount

d. With both objects still selected, from the Font Size drop-down list, **select 12.**

e. With both objects still selected, from the Border drop-down list, **select Top Border.**

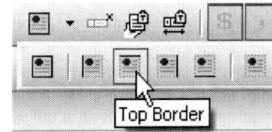

Top Border

f. **Deselect the two objects.**

g. To preview the grand total information, **select the Preview tab.**

3,148   06/20/04 $2,939.85
Group Total $2,939.85

Grand Total $3,982,734.36

h. **Observe the objects in the Report Footer section.** Notice that the grand total information is easy to distinguish from the surrounding data.

TOPIC D

Change Group Options

After grouping a report, you may want to modify the group's settings. In this topic, you will change group options.

After creating a group, the group may not display as you want. For example, you may decide that you want to change the field used to group the report, or you may want to change how the grouped field is sorted. You can make these and other changes using the Change Group Options dialog box.

How to Change Group Options

Procedure Reference: Change Group Options

To change group options:

1. On the Design tab, to the left of the report area, in the gray label area for the desired group, right-click and choose Change Group. The Change Group Options dialog box is displayed.

2. Select the desired group options.

   - To change the field used to group the report, on the Common tab, from the top drop-down list, select the new field.

   - To change the sort order for the field used to group the report, on the Common tab, from the second drop-down list, select the sort type.

   - To change the header displayed above each group, select the Options tab, check the Customize Group Name Field check box, and select the existing field that you want to appear in the header.

   - To prevent groups from breaking across pages, check the Keep Group Together check box. If necessary, the entire group may move to the following page so that all its contents remain together on the page. However, some groups may be too large to fit on a single page, and so must split across pages, even when you check the Keep Group Together check box.

     ✒ Use of the Keep Group Together check box can leave large gaps in a report.

   - To repeat the group header at the top of each page when a group is split across pages, check the Repeat Group Header On Each Page check box.

3. Click OK to apply the settings.

Procedure Reference: Adjust Section Height

To adjust the height of a section:

1. Position the mouse pointer anywhere along the section's bottom border and drag up or down.

   ✒ When you can increase an object's height, if necessary, the section's height will automatically increase to accommodate the object's new height.

ACTIVITY 3-4

Changing Group Options

Setup:
The grand total for the Customer Grouping.rpt report is displayed on the Preview tab.

Scenario:
After printing the report, you realize that it would be ideal to keep the data for each group together on one page. However, for cases in which the groups are longer than one page and are forced to display on multiple pages, you need the group header for each group to display at the top of each page.

What You Do	How You Do It
1. Preview the data for BBS Pty.	a. In the Group Tree, **click BBS Pty.**
	b. In the report's navigation buttons, **click the Show Next Page button and scroll to the top of page 2.**
	c. **Observe the BBS Pty data.** Notice that the customer's data is split over two pages.
2. Specify the group options.	a. **Display the Design tab.**
	b. In the gray area of the Group Header #1 section, **right-click and choose Change Group.**
	c. **Select the Options tab.**
	d. **Check the Keep Group Together check box.**
	e. **Check the Repeat Group Header On Each Page check box.**
	☑ Keep Group Together
	☑ Repeat Group Header On Each Page
	f. **Click OK.**

3. Adjust the Group #1 Name field so that it can display its contents fully.

a. **Increase the Group #1 Name field's width to 3.5″.**

b. **Increase the field's height by one-eighth of an inch.**

GH1	.	Group #1 Name	
D	.	Customer ID	Customer Name

c. **Observe the section's height.** It increases automatically to accommodate the taller field.

4. Preview the data for BBS Pty.

a. **Select the Preview tab.**

b. **Observe the BBS Pty data.** Notice that all of the customer's data is now displayed on page 2 of the report.

TOPIC E

Add a Second-Level Grouping

After creating a report that is grouped by a single field, you may want to further analyze the data. In this topic, you will add a second-level grouping to your report.

You want to further categorize grouped data in an employee report. In addition to grouping by department, you want to group it by hire year. You can create a group within a group to break down your data so that it is even easier to understand and is better organized.

How to Add a Second-Level Grouping

Procedure Reference: Add Groups

To add a second-level group to a report:

1. Display the Insert Group dialog box.
    - On the Insert Tools toolbar, click the Insert Group button.
    - Or, choose Insert→Group.

2. On the Common tab, from the top drop-down list, select the field by which you want to group the data.

3. From the second drop-down list, select the order by which you want to sort the group and click OK.

🔖 You can also use the Group Expert button to add an additional group to your report.

4. Arrange or remove groups as needed.
- To change a group header's position, select the Group Header field and press the arrow keys as needed. The amount of movement for each time an arrow key is pressed is determined by the field grid size.
- To rearrange the order of the groups, on the Design tab, hold down the mouse button on the gray area of the group header or group footer that you want to move and drag the section up or down.

🔖 To rearrange sub-sections, you can also display the Section Expert dialog box, select the sub-section you want to move, and use the Up Arrow or Down Arrow buttons.

- To delete a group, right-click the gray area of the group section and choose Delete Group.

ACTIVITY 3-5

Add a Second-Level Grouping

Setup:
Page 2 of the Customer Grouping.rpt report is displayed on the Preview tab.

Scenario:
To be able to analyze data within the groups even further, you need to add a second-level grouping to the report that groups Order Date by half year within each customer group. You then need to format the original group header information to stand out from the new group header information. Lastly, you want to experiment by changing the order of the groups so that the report is grouped by Order Date, and then by Customer Name.

What You Do	How You Do It
1. Group the report by Order Date for each half year in ascending order.	a. Select the Design tab.
	b. On the Insert Tools toolbar, **click the Insert Group button** 🔲.
	c. Set the option to group the report by the Orders.Order Date field in ascending order.

d. From the The Section Will Be Printed drop-down list, **select For Each Half Year.**

When the report is printed, the records will be sorted and grouped by:

▭ Orders.Order Date ⌄

in ascending order. ⌄

☐ Use a Formula as Group Sort Order   X-2

The section will be printed:

for each half year. ⌄

---

2. **Create the group so that a group header prints at the top of each page.**

a. **Display the Options tab.**

b. **Check the Repeat Group Header On Each Page check box.**

c. **Click OK.**

d. **Observe the report sections.** Notice that there are now additional Group Header #2 and Group Footer #2 sections.

e. **Select the Preview tab.**

Backpedal Cycle Shop

1/04		
46	Backpedal Cycle Shop
46	Backpedal Cycle Shop
46	Backpedal Cycle Shop

7/04		
46	Backpedal Cycle Shop
46	Backpedal Cycle Shop
46	Backpedal Cycle Shop

f. **Observe the second-level group.** Notice that the Group Header #2 formatting is identical to that of Group Header #1, and that the second group separates the orders in six-month increments.

---

3. Format Group Header #1.

    a. Display the Design tab.

    b. Select the Group #1 Name field.

    c. On the Formatting toolbar, from the Font Face drop-down list, **select Verdana.**

    d. On the Formatting toolbar, **click the Italics button** I.

---

4. **Indent the Group Header #2 field to the 0.25" mark.**

    a. In the Group Header #2 section, **select the Group #2 Name field.**

GH1	.	*Group #1 Name*
GH2	.	**Group #2 Nam e**
D	.	Customer ID

    b. To indent the selected field 0.25", **press the Right Arrow key three times.**

       ⚠️ If the field does not move using the arrow key, you can drag the associated guideline or drag the field to the 0.25" mark.

    c. **Select the Preview tab.**

Backpedal Cycle Shop

1/04
46	Backpedal Cycle Shop
46	Backpedal Cycle Shop
46	Backpedal Cycle Shop

7/04
46	Backpedal Cycle Shop
46	Backpedal Cycle Shop
46	Backpedal Cycle Shop

    d. **Observe the new formatting.** Notice that the Group Header #1 heading is now set in a new italicized font and the Group Header #2 heading has been indented.

---

5. **Reverse the group order.**

    a. **Select the Design tab.**

b. **Place the mouse pointer over the gray Group Header #1 area and hold down the mouse button.**

GH1 ✋	·	Group #1 Name
GH2	·	Group #2 Name
D	·	Customer ID
GF2	·	
GF1	·	

c. The mouse pointer changes to a hand and the Group Header #1 and Group Footer #1 sections are highlighted. **Drag down until a highlighted box is displayed around the Details section.**

d. **Release the mouse button.**

GH1	·	Group #1 Name
GH2	·	Group #2 Name
D	·	Customer ID
GF2	·	
GF1	·	

e. **Select the Preview tab.**

f. **Observe the reorganized groups.** Notice that first-half orders are grouped together for all customers.

1/03	
Pathfinders	
2	Pathfinders
Pedals Inc.	
28	Pedals Inc.
28	Pedals Inc.

g. The new group order does not make the data easier to analyze. **Click the Undo button** ↺ ▾.

TOPIC F

Filter Records by Group

You have reviewed many options for changing the display of your report data using groups, including formatting group headers and changing the group order. Another option you might want to use is to display only certain records in a group. In this topic, you will filter records within a group.

When you group or summarize data in a report, all the grouped data is included in the report. However, at times you may want to display only some of the records within the group. Filtering records in a group enables you to further specify and identify desired records.

Formulas

The purpose of a *formula* is to perform operations on data. The equation can be used to perform mathematical operations, such as addition or subtraction, or it can be used to compare, join, or extract data. In Crystal Reports, a formula consists of two parts: components and syntax.

Components, Operators, and Syntax

Components are the parts of the formula. When you create a formula, you can include:

- Fields
- Numbers
- Text
- *Operators*
- Functions
- Control structures
- Group field values
- Other formulas

Syntax refers to the rules that you must follow when organizing the components of a formula. Some of the basic rules you must follow in Crystal Reports include the following:

- Text strings must be enclosed in quotation marks.
- Arguments must be enclosed in parentheses, when necessary.
- Referenced formulas must be identified using a leading @ sign.

Operators and Control Structures

Operators are the actions you can use in your formulas, such as add (+) and subtract (–), to specify the type of calculation that you want to perform. Control structures are a way to express business logic, such as "If."

Types of Syntax

When you create formulas in Crystal Reports, you can use either Crystal syntax or Basic syntax. A report can include formulas that use both types of syntax, but Basic syntax and Crystal syntax cannot be mixed within the same formula.

Types of Formulas in Crystal Reports

You can create four different types of formulas in Crystal Reports. Most of the formulas that you will create will either be report or *conditional formatting* formulas.

Formula Type	Function
Report	A formula that stands alone in a report.
Conditional Formatting	A formula that changes the layout and design of a report based on specific criteria—for example, applying italic formatting to records representing sales from Region B. You create the formula using the Format Editor to access the Formula Editor.
Selection	A formula that specifies and limits the records and groups that are displayed in a report. You normally create the formula using the Select Expert.
Search	A formula used to locate data in a report. You normally create the formula by using the Search Expert.

Selection Formulas

One purpose of a group selection formula is to filter data by group. A *selection formula* is a filter used to limit the data included in a report. Selection formulas can be created at the record or the group level.

How to Filter Records by Group

Procedure Reference: Filter by Group

To filter a report by group:

1. Select the group field for which you want to create a filter.

    > Filtering by group is very much like filtering data using a single criterion. So, these steps may be familiar to you.

2. Display the Select Expert dialog box.
    - On the Expert Tools toolbar, click the Select Expert button.
    - Choose Report→Select Expert.
    - Or, right-click the group field and choose Select Expert.

3. On the field's tab, from the drop-down list, select the appropriate comparison operator, or click Show Formula and type one manually in the text box.

4. From the second drop-down list, select a value, or enter a value manually in the drop-down list.

5. Click OK to filter the report by the selected group.

ACTIVITY 3-6

Filtering by Group

Setup:
Page 2 of the Customer Grouping.rpt report is displayed on the Preview tab.

Scenario:
To help increase company sales, the marketing department would like to contact all customers who have placed orders totalling $1,000 or less. There are 48 or so pages of customers and order amounts you need to organize based on this criteria.

What You Do	How You Do It
1. Display the Select Expert dialog box for the Order Amount field.	a. Select the Design tab.
	b. In the Group Footer #1 section, **select the Sum Of Orders.Order Amount field.**
	c. On the Expert Tools toolbar, **click the Select Expert button** .
	d. **Click Show Formula.**
	e. **Notice that the Group Selection option is selected.** This is because you selected a group field.
	f. **Click Hide Formula.**
2. Create a group selection formula for the Sum Of Orders.Order Amount field that displays those groups with an order total that is less than or equal to $1,000.	a. On the Sum Of Orders.Order Amount tab, from the drop-down list, **select Is Less Than Or Equal To.**
	b. In the second drop-down list, **type *1000* and click OK.**

3.	Display the last page of the filtered group report.	a.	Select the Preview tab.
		b.	In the navigation buttons, **click the Show Last Page button.**
		c.	**Observe the total number of pages displayed.** The report now only displays those customers who have made total purchases of less than $1,000.

TOPIC G

Create a Top N Sort Group

You have filtered records in groups. However, you may want to view only the top data groupings based on summarized data for each group. In this topic, you will display specified groups using a Top N sort group.

You want to display only the group of employees hired in a single year who have the highest combined salary for each department. Using the Top N sort group, you can easily display only those employee records you specify.

Top N Sort Group

At some point, you might want to display only the top groups in a report—for example, the top three regions that produce the most orders. You can use the Sort Group Expert for displaying that group information. The Top N sort group is available only in reports that have summary fields.

Remove Grand Totals

Grand totals are calculated before a Top N sort and group filter is applied and will, therefore, be incorrect. Grand totals should be removed from Top N sort and group reports. As an alternative, they can be manually created using variables in Running Total fields, which goes beyond the scope of this course.

Group Sort Options

Besides Top N, you have other group sort options:

- No Sort
- All
- Bottom N
- Top Percentage
- Bottom Percentage

How to Create a Top N Sort Group

Procedure Reference: Create a Top N Sort Group

To create a Top N sort group:

1. Delete any existing selection formula as necessary so that the data displays the way you want it to.
   a. Display the Select Expert dialog box.
   b. Select the tab that contains the selection formula that you want to delete.
   c. Click Delete to delete the selection formula.
   d. Click OK to close the Select Expert dialog box.

2. Display the Group Sort Expert dialog box.
   - On the Expert Tools toolbar, click the Group Sort Expert button.
   - Or, choose Report→Group Sort Expert.

3. From the For This Group Sort drop-down list, select Top N.

4. In the Where N Is text box, type the number of Top N values that you want to display.

5. If desired, uncheck the Include Others, With The Name check box so that the other records do not display.

6. Click OK to create the group.

ACTIVITY 3-7

Creating a Top N Sort Group

Setup:

The last page of the Customer Grouping.rpt report is displayed on the Preview tab.

Scenario:

The customer service director wants to send a special gift to the customers with the top five order amounts, and has asked you to identify those customers in a report.

What You Do	How You Do It
1. Remove the selection formula for the Sum Of Orders.Order Amount field.	a. On the Expert Tools toolbar, **click the Select Expert button** 🔍.
	b. In the Select Expert dialog box, **select the Sum Of Orders.Order Amount tab.**
	c. **Click Delete and click OK.**
	d. When prompted, **click Refresh Data.**

2. **Create a Top N sort group.**

a. On the Expert Tools toolbar, **click the Group Sort Expert button** 📉.

b. From the For This Group Sort drop-down list, **select Top N.**

c. The Based On drop-down list contains the Sum Of Orders.Order Amount field, as that is the only summary you have created for that group. In the Where N Is text box, **verify that 5 is displayed and that the Include Others, With The Name check box is unchecked.**

Customer.Customer Name

For this group sort

| Top N ▾ | based on | Sum of Orders.Order Amount |

Where N is:

5   ✕2

☐ Include Others, with the name:

Others

d. **Click OK.**

e. **Observe the Group Tree.** Notice that the top five customers are listed and that Psycho-Cycle has purchased the most.

3. **Save and close the report.**

Lesson 3 Follow-up

In this lesson, you grouped and summarized data in a report. By grouping and summarizing similar data, your reports will be better organized and the information will be more meaningful to your audience.

1. **What types of summaries will you add to your reports?**

2. **In grouped reports, how might you change the display of the groups and the group headers?**

3. **Based on your typical reporting requirements, what types of Top N sort groups will you create?**

NOTES

LESSON 4
Building Formulas

Lesson Time
*2 hour(s) to 2 hour(s),
30 minutes*

Lesson Objectives:

In this lesson, you will build formulas to calculate and display data.

You will:

- Create a formula that calculates field data.

- Edit a formula.

- Display groups based on a formula.

- Delete a formula.

- Create a formula that filters data based on several conditions.

- Modify a filter using an OR operator.

- Create a parameter field.

- Create a formula that accounts for null values.

Introduction

You have created some reports that contain data that you have obtained from a database. At some point, you may want to create calculated fields from the data. In this lesson, you will build formulas that allow you to add calculated data to your reports.

Using formulas, you can enhance your reports by adding calculated fields that are not available in the database.

TOPIC A

Create a Formula

You have added fields to reports by using tables that exist in a database. You need to display data in a report that is derived from that data, but it is not directly available in the database. In this topic, you will create a formula to display such data.

You want to display the total cost of units sold per customer. You do not have a database field containing that amount. You only have unit price and quantity fields. To obtain the total cost, you could create a formula that multiplies the unit price by the quantity; thereby adding data to a report that cannot be obtained directly from a database.

Operators

There are many different operators that you can use in your reports to calculate the components of formulas. See Table 4-1 for examples.

Table 4-1: *Operators*

Operator	Description
Addition (+)	**Definition:** Adds values. **Example:** 6+7
Subtraction (-)	**Definition:** Subtracts values. **Example:** 197-113
Multiplication (*)	**Definition:** Multiplies values. **Example:** 12*12
Division (/)	**Definition:** Divides values. **Example:** 36/6
Equal	**Definition:** x is equal to y. **Example:** {Orders.Quantity}=7
Less than	**Definition:** x is less than y. **Example:** {Orders.Quantity}<50
Greater than	**Definition:** x is greater than y. **Example:** {Orders.Quantity}>50
Concatenate (&)	**Definition:** Combines values. **Example:** {FirstName}&{LastName}
And	**Definition:** Includes the values x and y. **Example:** {Orders.Quantity}=50 and {Orders.Salesperson}="PS"
Or	**Definition:** Includes the value x or y. **Example:** {Orders.Quantity}=50 or {Orders.Salesperson}="PS"

Operator	Description
If-then-else	**Definition:** If the statement following the word IF is true, return what comes after the THEN statement; otherwise, return what comes after the ELSE statement. **Example:** If {Employee.Dept}="Northeast" Then {Employee.Salary}*.08 Else {Employee.Salary}*.06

Order of Operations

When you create or edit a formula, the formula might contain more than one arithmetic expression that contains several operators. In that case, the order of operations becomes a factor. Crystal Reports typically evaluates formulas in the following order:

1. From left to right.

2. Then, follows the order of operations rule from basic math (multiplication and division are performed first from left to right, and then addition and subtraction are performed from left to right).

While most formulas are evaluated from left to right, evaluation time statements and the type of formula can cause evaluation to occur earlier or later. See the Report Processing Model topic in Crystal Reports' Online Help.

The order of operations can be changed by adding parentheses. The following list displays the arithmetic operators from highest precedence to lowest:

1. Exponentiation (^)

2. Negation (-)

3. Multiplication and division (*, /)

4. Integer division (\)

5. Modulus (Mod)

6. Addition and subtraction (+, -)

Formula Workshop

When you create and edit a formula, you will use the Formula Workshop, which is where you can access and modify all the formulas. Figure 4-1 displays an example of the Formula Workshop interface.

If you change the syntax from Crystal to Basic or vice versa, the list of functions and operators will change.

Component	Function
Workshop Tree	Contains folders for each type of formula you can create in Crystal Reports, along with folders for creating custom functions and SQL Expressions.
Expression Editor toolbar	Includes buttons that help you write and navigate your formulas.

Component	Function
Save toolbar	Includes buttons for saving formulas.
General toolbar	Includes buttons that help you create formulas, and that show or hide certain workshop components.
Workshop Tree toolbar	Includes buttons that help you modify and organize your custom formulas.
Report Fields tree	A component of the Formula Editor window, it contains all database fields available in the report, and formulas and groups already created in the report.
Functions tree	A component of the Formula Editor window, it contains the functions you can use to create formulas.
Operators tree	A component of the Formula Editor window, it contains the operators you can use to create formulas.
Formula Text window	A component of the Formula Editor window, it is the area you use to create and edit the formula.

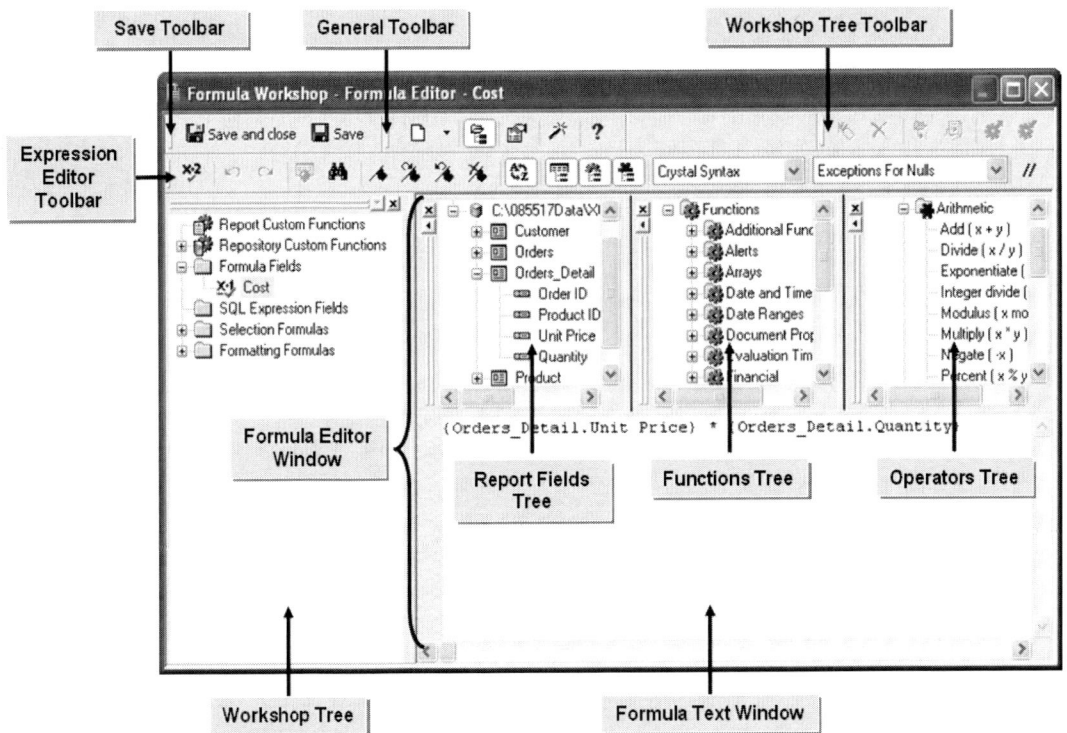

Figure 4-1: *Components of the Formula Workshop.*

Formula Editor

The Formula Editor window is the primary formula editor, which contains the Report Fields tree, Functions tree, Operators tree, and Formula Text window.

How to Create a Formula

Procedure Reference: Write a Formula

To create a formula:

1. If necessary, display the Field Explorer.

    - On the Standard toolbar, click the Field Explorer button.

    - Or, choose View→Field Explorer.

2. In the list, select Formula Fields.

    If desired, you can type the components of the formula in the Formula Text window.

3. On the Field Explorer toolbar, click the New button to display the Formula Name dialog box.

4. In the Name text box, type a name for your formula and click OK.

5. In the Formula Text window, in the associated tree, enter the components of the formula by double-clicking, dragging, or typing the components.

6. On the Expression Editor toolbar, click the Check button to check for errors in the formula. A message box is displayed indicating whether or not there are errors in the formula.

    If an error is found, Crystal Reports will try to determine the cause of the error and place the insertion point in that position.

7. If there are errors in the formula, you must close the message box and resolve the errors.

8. When the formula is error free, click OK to close the message box.

9. On the Save toolbar, click Save to save the formula, or click Save And Close to save the formula and close the Formula Workshop.

10. From the Field Explorer, drag the formula field to the desired location within the report.

11. If desired, preview the report.

ACTIVITY 4-1

Writing a Formula

Data Files:

- Customer Order Totals.rpt

Setup:

No files are open in Crystal Reports. The Start Page is displayed.

Scenario:

You have created a report named Customer Order Totals that summarizes the order information for each customer. You want the report to include the order total. However, the database that you used to create the report does not include that field.

What You Do	How You Do It
1. Open the Customer Order Totals.rpt report in Design view.	a. Open the Customer Order Totals.rpt report.
	b. Select the Design tab.

2.	**Display the Formula Workshop for the new formula, Order Total.**	a. If necessary, on the Standard toolbar, **click the Field Explorer button** 🎞️.
		b. In the Field Explorer, from the list, **select Formula Fields.**
		c. On the Field Explorer toolbar, **click the New button** 🖼️.
		d. In the Name text box, **type** *Order Total*
		e. To display the Formula Editor, **click OK.**
3.	**Insert the components for the Order Total formula.**	a. In the Report Fields tree, **expand C:\085517\Xtreme.mdb.**
		b. In the Report Fields tree, **expand the Orders_Detail table.**
		c. In the Report Fields tree, to place the field in the Formula Text window, **double-click Unit Price.**
		d. You will now add the operator for multi-plication. In the Operators tree, **expand the Operators folder and the Arithmetic folder, and then double-click Multiply (x * y).**
		e. In the Report Fields tree, **double-click Quantity.**

```
{Orders_Detail.Unit Price} * {Orders_Detail.Quantity}
```

LESSON 4

4. **Check the formula for errors, save, and close the Formula Workshop.**

   a. On the Expression Editor toolbar, **click the Check button** ⊡.

   b. No errors are found. **Click OK.**

   c. On the Formula Workshop's Save toolbar, **click Save And Close.**

---

5. **Insert the Order Total formula to the right of the Quantity field, and preview the report.**

   a. From the Field Explorer, **drag the Order Total formula to the right of the Quantity field in the Details section.**

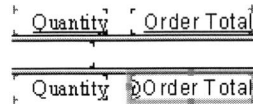

   b. **Select the Preview tab.**

   c. To hide the Group Tree, on the Standard toolbar, **click the Toggle Group Tree button** ▦.

   d. **Observe the Order Total for AIC Childrens.** The Order Total ($101.70) equals the Unit Price ($33.90) multiplied by the Quantity (3). Also, the font for the Order Total field is Arial, while all other fields are Times New Roman.

---

6. Using the Design tab, **change the font for all fields and field labels to Arial.**	a. **Select the Design tab.**
	b. **Choose Edit→Select All.**
	c. From the Font Face drop-down list, **select Arial.**
	d. **Select the Preview tab.**
	e. **Observe the Order Total field.** All other fields now match the Order Total field's font.

TOPIC B

Edit a Formula

After creating a formula, you may not be getting the results you intended. As a result, you will need to modify the formula. In this topic, you will edit a formula.

You create a formula and later find that it is missing a component. You can easily add that component to the formula. Editing an existing formula is easier than starting over.

How to Edit a Formula

Procedure Reference: Edit a Formula

To edit a formula:

1. If necessary, display the Field Explorer.

2. Under the Formula Fields category, select the formula you want to edit.

3. Display the Formula Workshop.
   - Click the Edit button.
   - Or, right-click the formula in the report and choose Edit.

4. Edit the formula as needed.

5. Check the formula for errors.

6. Save the formula and close the Formula Workshop.

ACTIVITY 4-2

Editing a Formula

Setup:

The first page of the Customer Order Totals.rpt report is displayed on the Preview tab. The Group Tree is hidden.

Scenario:

After previewing the Customer Order Totals report, you realize that each order total needs to include the company's standard $10.95 shipping charge.

What You Do	How You Do It
1. Add the shipping charge to the formula.	a. In the Field Explorer, **select the Order Total formula.**
	b. On the Field Explorer toolbar, to display the Formula Workshop, **click the Edit button** .
	c. In the Formula Text window, **place the insertion point at the end of the formula.**
	d. In the Operators tree, below Arithmetic, **double-click Add (x + y).**
	e. **Type 10.95**
2. Check for errors and save your changes.	a. **Click the Check button** .
	b. No errors are found. **Click OK.**
	c. **Click Save And Close.**
	d. **Observe the Order Total for AIC Childrens.** The formula is calculated from left to right. The Order Total ($112.65) equals the Unit Price ($33.90) multiplied by the Quantity (3) plus the $10.95 standard shipping charge.

TOPIC C

Combine Fields by Formula

In addition to creating basic mathematical formulas, you might need to create formulas that allow you to combine more than one field. In this topic, you will combine fields using formulas.

You have an employee sales report grouped by last name so that you can display the total quarter sales for each employee. However, two employees have the same last name, so their records are grouped and summarized together. Combining the first and last name fields using a formula will allow you to group and summarize the records for each salesperson.

ToText Function

The ToText function will convert a Number, Currency, Date, Time, or DateTime value to a text string so that it is displayed as text in the report. This can be useful for removing decimal digits typically generated for numeric values displayed in number fields.

How to Combine Fields by Formula

Procedure Reference: Group by Formula

To group a report by using a formula:

1. If necessary, display the Field Explorer and create a new formula with a name of your choice.

2. In the Formula Workshop, enter the formula components.

   a. To combine two fields using a formula, add the first field.

   b. Before inserting other fields or characters that you want to combine, type the ampersand character (&).

   c. Type any text characters, including spaces between fields, within quotation marks.

   d. Insert the second field.

3. Check the formula for errors.

4. Save and close the formula and the Formula Workshop.

5. Using the Change Group Options dialog box, change the field for sorting and grouping the report using your new formula.

Procedure Reference: Prevent Decimal Digits from Being Displayed

If one of the fields you have combined includes numbers that display decimal digits, and you do not want the decimal digits to display, you can modify the formula to remove the decimal digits. To prevent decimal digits from being displayed:

1. In the Field Explorer, select the formula that displays decimal digits and click the Edit button.

2. Place the insertion point before the opening { character at the beginning of the field and type ToText(.

3. Place the insertion point after the field's closing } character and type ,0).

4. Verify that the field appears as ToText({fieldname},0).

5. Save the formula and close the Formula Workshop.

ACTIVITY 4-3

Grouping by Formula

Setup:

The Customer Order Totals.rpt report is displayed on the Preview tab. The Field Explorer is also displayed.

Scenario:

In the event that a customer has two locations, each requiring its own customer ID, the Customer Order Totals report can't provide the detail by location because the report is grouped currently by customer name; therefore, additional locations, even with unique customer numbers, would still be grouped and summarized together with locations using the same customer name.

What You Do	How You Do It
1. Display the Formula Workshop for a new formula named *Group Sort*.	a. In the Field Explorer, **verify that Formula Fields is selected and click the New button.**
	b. **Name the formula *Group Sort***
	c. **Click OK.**
2. Create the formula.	a. In the Report Fields tree, **expand the Customer table.**
	b. In the Report Fields tree, **double-click Customer Name.**
	c. To string together the Customer.Customer Name field with a space and an opening parenthesis, **type &" and press the Spacebar. Then, type ("**
	d. To prepare to string the Customer Name field with the Customer ID field, **type &**
	e. In the Customer table, **double-click the Customer ID field.**

f. To string the closing parenthesis with the
    Customer ID field, **type &")"**

`{Customer.Customer Name}&" ("&{Customer.Customer ID}&")"`

---

3. **Complete the formula.**

a. **Click the Check button.**

b. No errors are found. **Click OK.**

c. On the Formula Workshop's Save toolbar,
    click Save And Close.

---

4. **Change the existing group so that
    the report is grouped by the Group
    Sort formula.**

a. **Select the Design tab.**

b. In the gray area of the Group Header #1
    section, **right-click and choose Change
    Group.**

c. On the Common tab, **sort and group the
    report in ascending order using the
    Group Sort formula and click OK.**

d. **Select the Preview tab.**

e. **Observe the Group Header #1 field.**
    Notice that the Company Name data pre-
    cedes the Customer ID data, which is in
    parentheses. However, the Customer ID
    number includes unnecessary decimal
    places.

---

5. **Modify the formula so that the Cus-
    tomer ID data is displayed without
    decimal places.**

a. In the Field Explorer, **select the Group
    Sort formula.**

b. **Click the Edit button.**

c. Before the Customer ID field, **place the
    insertion point between the second &
    character and the { character.**

`Name}&" ("&{Customer`

d. **Type ToText(**

e. After the Customer ID field, **place the insertion point after the } character.**

```
("&ToText({Customer.Customer ID}&")"
```

f. **Type ,0)**

6. **Preview the report.**

a. **Click the Check button.**

b. No errors are found. **Click OK.**

c. **Click Save And Close.**

d. **Observe the Group Header #1 field.** Notice that the Customer ID data no longer includes unnecessary decimal places.

TOPIC D

Delete a Formula

As you add multiple formulas to a report, you might have a formula in a report that you no longer need. In this topic, you will delete a formula.

Deleting unneeded formulas removes excess clutter from the Field Explorer, allowing you to more easily locate the formulas you need.

How to Delete a Formula

Procedure Reference: Delete a Formula

To delete a formula from a report:

1. If applicable, select the formula field and its label in the report.

2. Press Delete. If applicable, remove all references to the formula in other report locations (select expert formulas, grouping formulas, or conditional format formulas).

3. Display the Field Explorer and, if necessary, expand Formula Fields.

4. Select the formula you want to delete.

5. Delete the formula.

    • On the Field Explorer toolbar, click the Delete button.

- Press Delete on the keyboard.

- Or, right-click the formula and choose Delete.

🖉 If you delete a formula in the Field Explorer and that formula is located somewhere else in the report, a warning message will be displayed.

Potential Issues When Deleting Formulas

Formulas used for display purposes can easily be removed from a report by simply deleting the formula from the Field Explorer. Deleting the formula field from the Field Explorer will also remove the formulas from the report.

However, if the formula field is used to filter, group, or conditionally format data, deleting the formula becomes a two-step process. In that case, you cannot delete the formula from the Field Explorer without first deleting every occurrence of the formula in the report.

As a general rule, it is good practice to remove all occurrences of a formula before removing it from the Field Explorer window since this would alert you to any "hidden" places where the formula might reside.

ACTIVITY 4-4

Deleting a Formula

Setup:

The Customer Order Totals.rpt report is displayed on the Preview tab. The Field Explorer is also displayed.

Scenario:

You no longer need the Order Total formula field in your report. The Order Total formula field is used in the report, as indicated in the Field Explorer, by the check mark on the field icon.

What You Do	How You Do It
1. Delete the Order Total formula from the report layout.	a. Select the Design tab.
	b. Select the @Order Total field and its label.
	c. Press Delete.
	d. Observe the Order Total in the Field Explorer. Notice that the icon no longer displays a check mark.

2. **Delete the Order Total formula from the report file.**

a. In the Field Explorer, **select Order Total.**

b. On the Field Explorer toolbar, **click the Delete button** ⊠.

c. **Select the Preview tab.**

d. **Observe the report.** Notice that the Order Total field is no longer displayed in the report, nor is it displayed in the Field Explorer.

TOPIC E

Filter Data by Multiple Criteria

Another way to affect the display of data in your reports is to use a formula that filters data based on more than one field. In this topic, you will use a formula to filter records based on multiple criteria.

You want to filter records based on the contents of more than one field. By creating a formula, you can accomplish that task. Only the data that you want to view will be displayed, saving you the aggravation of having to work with more data than you need. Also, the report will be easier to read because less data is displayed.

The AND Operator

You can create a formula that filters a report based on more than one field, so that all components of the formula must be true. This is accomplished by using the AND operator to separate the filter criteria. When AND is used in a selection formula, the data extracted must meet all conditions of the criteria.

How to Filter Data by Multiple Criteria

Procedure Reference: Filter Data Using Multiple Criteria

To use a formula that filters data based on multiple criteria:

1. Select the first report field on which you want to filter.

2. Display the Select Expert dialog box.
   - On the Expert Tools toolbar, click the Select Expert button.
   - Choose Report→Select Expert.
   - Or, right-click and choose Select Expert.

3. From the drop-down list, select the appropriate comparison operator, or click Show Formula and type one in the text box.

4. In the second drop-down list, type or select a value.

5. Select the New tab and choose a new field.

6. Repeat steps 3 and 4.

7. Click OK to filter the data.

8. If necessary, refresh the data.

ACTIVITY 4-5

Building a Filter Using Multiple Criteria

Setup:

The Customer Order Totals.rpt report is displayed on the Preview tab.

Scenario:

The finance department needs to know what customers in Massachusetts placed orders between 1/1/2003 and 1/31/2003.

What You Do	How You Do It
1. Create the first part of the selection formula that will display those customers equal to MA.	a. Select the Design tab.
	b. In the Details section, **select the Customer.Region field and click the Select Expert button.**
	c. On the Customer.Region tab, **set the comparison operator to Is Equal To.**
	d. In the second drop-down list, **type MA**

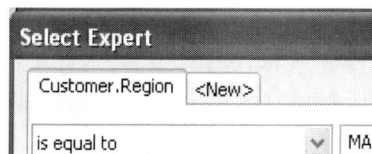

LESSON 4.

2. **Create the second part of the selection formula.**

   a. **Select the New tab.**

   b. To choose a field, **double-click Orders.Order Date.**

   c. On the Orders.Order Date tab, **set the comparison operator to Is Between.**

   d. In the second drop-down list, **type *1/1/ 2004* and press Tab.**

   e. In the third drop-down list, **type *1/31/ 2004***

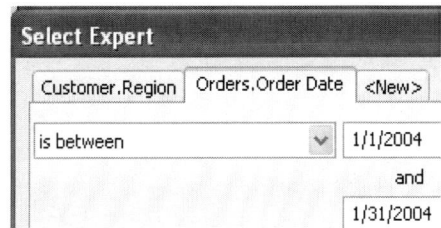

   f. **Click Show Formula.**

```
{Customer.Region} = "MA" and
{Orders.Order Date} in Date (2004, 01, 01) to Date (2004, 01, 31)
```

   g. **Observe the formula.** Notice that the two criteria are connected by the word "and."

   h. **Click OK.**

3. **Preview the report.**

   a. **Select the Preview tab.**

   b. When prompted, **click Refresh Data.**

   c. **Observe the report.** Notice that only two customers meet the specified criteria—Massachusetts customers who placed orders in January of 2004.

TOPIC F

Modify a Filter Using an OR Operator

Another way to affect the display of data in your reports using formulas is to create a filter that displays specified data that meets any one of multiple criteria. In this topic, you will modify a filter to include records that must meet only one of multiple criteria.

You have an employee salary report that contains a Department field, and you want to view all employee salary data for both the publishing and office support departments. An OR operator will allow you to display all records in the Department field that equals either publishing or office support.

How to Modify a Filter Using an OR Operator

Procedure Reference: Modify a Filter with Multiple Criteria to Include an OR Operator

To modify a formula that filters a report based on more than one criteria where the data must meet any one criterion:

1. Select the field that contains the formula to be modified and display the Select Expert dialog box.

    ✐ You can also locate all records that match any one of multiple criteria for a given field using the Is One Of operator in the Select Expert. However, using the Formula Workshop provides the most control, including access to all the formula components that you would need to build a complex formula.

2. Click Show Formula.

3. To display the Formula Workshop, click Formula Editor.

4. Modify the formula to add new conditions, separating each condition with the word "OR."

5. Check your formula for errors.

6. Save and close the formula.

7. If prompted, refresh the data.

    ✐ If you were to select Use Saved Data, processing would be much quicker, but that option would start with the current returned records and never go back to the database for other records. If the filter is intended to narrow the current recordset, you can safely use the Use Saved Data option. If the filter might broaden the search to include records not currently in the recordset, the Refresh Data option should be selected.

Activity 4-6

Modifying a Filter to Include an OR Operator

Setup:
The Customer Order Totals.rpt report is displayed on the Preview tab.

Scenario:
You created the report to show January 2004 sales from Massachusetts customers. The finance department now asks that the same report include California customer sales for the same time period. You need to modify the filter.

What You Do	How You Do It
1. Modify the selection formula to add customers equal to CA.	a. With the Customer.Region field still selected, **click the Select Expert button.**
	b. **Click Show Formula.**
	c. To display the Formula Workshop, **click Formula Editor.**
	d. In the Formula Text window, before the first occurrence of {Customer.Region}, **type (**
	e. **Place the insertion point at the end of the formula.**
	f. **Press the Spacebar and type OR{Customer.Region}="CA")**
	(Orders.Order Date) in Date (2004, 01, 01) to Date (2004, 01, 31) and ((Customer.Region) = "MA" OR(Customer.Region)="CA")

2. **Finish the formula and preview the report.**

    a. **Check the formula for errors.**

    b. **Click OK.**

    c. **Save the formula and close the Formula Workshop.**

    d. **Click OK.**

    e. **Click Refresh Data.**

    f. **In the report, scroll down to count how many customers from MA and CA placed orders in January 2004.**

3. **How many customers from MA and CA placed orders in January 2004?**

    a) 2

    b) 3

    c) 8

    d) 9

TOPIC G

Create a Parameter Field

In addition to creating a filter that limits the data in a report based on multiple fields, you can create a formula that limits the data based on user input. In this topic, you will create a parameter field that will customize the display of data based on how users respond to a specified question.

You have an employee salary report that you want to set up for a colleague who is not familiar with Crystal Reports but who will need to view all records for a single department at a time. Creating a parameter field enables you to empower users to customize a report to meet their own needs.

How to Create a Parameter Field

Procedure Reference: Create a Parameter Field

A parameter field displays a dialog box that prompts users to enter or select values they want to view. To create a parameter field for use in a selection formula:

1. If necessary, select the Design tab, and display the Field Explorer.

2. In the Field Explorer, select Parameter Fields and click New. The Create Parameter Field dialog box is displayed.

3. In the Name text box, type a name for the parameter field.

4. If necessary, from the Type drop-down list, select the value type that matches your parameter field. Note that if you are going to reference the parameter in a selection formula, the two must be the same value type.

5. Select whether the List Of Values should be Static (the default) or Dynamic.

6. From the Value Field drop-down list, select the database field that will supply the list values.

7. If applicable, select a database field that helps to describe the database field you chose for the value.

8. From the Actions drop-down list, select Append All Database Values.

9. If desired, set parameter value options.
   - Prompt Text: Text that instructs users to perform a desired action.
   - Allow Multiple Values: Allows report users to select more than one value.
   - Allow Discrete Values: Allows report users to select one value.
   - Allow Range Values: Allows report users to select a range of values.

   Depending upon the parameter type you are creating, the parameter value options may vary.

10. Click OK to close the Create Parameter Field dialog box.

11. If desired, place the parameter field in the desired section to display the parameter field in the report itself. However, you do not have to display the parameter field in the report for it to function.

12. Display the Select Expert dialog box for the field on which the parameter field is based.

13. Set the desired comparison operator.

14. From the second drop-down list, select the parameter field and click OK. If your parameter field is not displayed in the drop-down list, the data type of the field selected does not match the data type chosen for your parameter field. Edit your parameter field formula to modify the value type.

15. Preview the report. The Enter Values dialog box is displayed.

16. Select the appropriate value and click OK, and then refresh the data to display the specified records.

17. To specify a different value for the parameter field so that it generates a different set of records, on the Standard toolbar, refresh the data and specify the new parameter value.
    a. Using the navigation buttons on the Preview tab, click the Refresh button.
    b. In the Refresh Report Data dialog box, select Prompt For New Parameter Values and click OK.
    c. In the Enter Values dialog box, provide a new value and click OK.

ACTIVITY 4-7

Creating a Parameter Field

Setup:
The Customer Order Totals.rpt report is displayed on the Preview tab.

Scenario:
The customer service manager would like to use your Customer Order Totals report daily in his department. However, he wants the report to be updated so the users of the report can display only the customers in one region at a time, which is the information they will need to answer customer questions.

What You Do	How You Do It
1. Name a new parameter field *Select Region*.	a. Select the Design tab.
	b. In the Field Explorer, **select Parameter Fields.**
	c. **Click New.**
	d. In the Name text box, **type *Select Region***
	e. In the Type drop-down list, **verify that String is selected.**
	f. **Verify that the List Of Values option is set to Static.**

2. **Add all Region data from the Customer table.**

   a. From the Value Field drop-down list, under Customer, **select Region.**

   b. To populate the Value list, from the Actions drop-down list, **select Append All Database Values.**

   c. In the Options list, **click in the Prompt Text text box and type** *Select a Region*

   d. To require users to select from the provided list, from the Allow Custom Values drop-down list, **select False.**

   e. **Click OK.**

3. **Place the parameter field in the Page Footer and make the field bold.**

   a. On the Design tab, from the Field Explorer, **drag the Select Region parameter field to the left side of the Page Footer section.**

   b. **Bold the Select Region parameter field.**

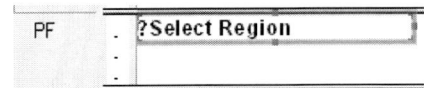

4. Is it necessary to place the parameter field within the layout for it to function?

5. **Create a selection formula that sets the Region field equal to the Select Region parameter field.**

   a. In the Details section, **select the Region field and display the Select Expert dialog box.**

   b. On the Customer.Region tab, **set the comparison operator to Is Equal To.**

c. From the second drop-down list, **select {?Select Region}.**

| Customer.Region | Orders.Order Date | <New> |

| is equal to ▾ | {?Select Region} |

d. **Click OK.**

---

6. **Display customers from Alabama using refreshed data.**

a. To display the Enter Values dialog box, **select the Preview tab.**

b. From the Select A Region drop-down list, **select AL and click OK.**

c. So that the report applies the selected parameter, **click Refresh Data.**

d. **Observe the report.** Notice that there is only one customer from Alabama.

e. **Scroll to the bottom of the page.**

f. **Observe the Report Footer area.** Notice that the Select Region parameter field is displayed.

---

7. **Display orders for customers from California and close the report.**

a. On the Navigation Tools toolbar, **click the Refresh button** .

b. In the Refresh Report Data dialog box, **select the Prompt For New Parameter Values option and click OK.**

c. In the Enter Values dialog box, from the Select A Region drop-down list, **select CA and click OK.**

d. **Scroll to the bottom of the page.**

e. **Observe the report.** Notice that there are six customers from California and that CA is now displayed in the Select Region parameter field.

---

8. Save and close the Customer Order Total report.

TOPIC H

Account for Null Fields in a Formula

Another type of formula you might need to create is one that deals with empty database fields. In this topic, you will write a formula that takes empty fields into account.

When working with database fields, at some point you will encounter fields that are empty. You can create a formula that incorporates empty fields, allowing you to display the records you need, even those with fields that include no values.

Nulls

The purpose of a null is to indicate fields that contain no data. Fields can be null if a field was never given a value. A field containing the number 0 is not considered a null field, since it contains data.

Issues with Nulls in Crystal Reports

A common problem with null values in Crystal Reports is that if a null field value is concatenated with another field value, the resulting formula will be null. For example, if you were to write a formula that strings together the first name, middle initial, and last name fields, no name would display at all if the middle initial was missing. One solution to this involves using the IsNull function in the formula creation.

Another common problem with null values is found when setting filter criteria. If a user wants to see all records where the order quantity was less than 5, for example, simply writing a formula {Orders.OrderQuantity} < 5 will not return the records where the order quantity is null. Changing the formula to read IsNull({Orders.OrderQuantity} OR {Orders.OrderQuantity}<5 would include the null records.

Functions That Account for Nulls

You can use a variety of functions to deal with null values when you are creating formulas.

Function	Description
If-Then-Else	If-Then-Else formulas perform a test on a database field, formula, or both. An example of an If statement might look like the following: `If x (the test) Then y (the result if true) Else z (the result if false)` In all If-Then-Else statements, the value for *y* and *z* must be the same data type.

Function	Description
IsNull	The IsNull function will test for the existence of a null value, returning true if a null value is found in the field following the function. For example, the formula `IsNull({Orders.OrderAmount})` would return true if the field was null, and false if there was a value in the field.
ToText	The ToText function will convert a Number, Currency, Date, Time, or DateTime value to a text string so that it is displayed as text in the report. The ToText function can be useful in conjunction with If-Then-Else statements, because the values returned in an If-Then-Else statement must always be the same data type. If there is a need to mix numbers with text, the ToText function will facilitate this. For example, if X was a number field, you might use the following formula to show X when it is not null and to display "N/A" if X is null: If IsNull(X) Then "N/A" Else ToText(X,0).
Abs	When you want to display a data value as an absolute value, without an indication of whether the number is negative or positive, you can specify the absolute value function, which appears as `Abs({Field Name})`. The Abs function is a Math function.

How to Account for Null Fields in a Formula

Procedure Reference: Write a Formula That Accounts for Null Fields

To create a formula that tests for null values, replacing a null value with x:

1. If necessary, display the Field Explorer and select Formula Fields.

2. On the Field Explorer toolbar, click the New button to display the Formula Name dialog box.

3. In the Name text box, type a name for your formula and click OK to display the Formula Workshop.

4. In the Formula Text window, enter the components of the formula. Include an If-Then-Else function and IsNull function where appropriate—for example, If IsNull({field being tested}) Then X Else Y.

5. Check for and correct errors in the formula.

6. Save the formula and close the Formula Workshop.

7. Using the Field Explorer, place the formula field in the appropriate location in your report.

8. If desired, preview the report.

ACTIVITY **4-8**

Writing a Formula That Incorporates Null Fields

Data Files:

- Customer Credit.rpt

Setup:

No files are open in Crystal Reports. The Start Page is displayed.

Scenario:

A coworker is learning how to use Crystal Reports, and she just created her first report called Customer Credit.rpt. However, she is having trouble with the way negative numbers and null fields are being displayed. She wants negative numbers to be displayed as positive numbers, and if a customer has no credits, the Credit Amount field should state "No Credits."

What You Do	How You Do It
1. In the Customer Credit report, create a formula named *AbsCredit* that returns the absolute value of the Credit.Amount field.	a. Open the Customer Credit.rpt report.
	b. Observe the data displayed in the Amount column. Notice that negative numbers are indicated by parentheses.

Customer Name and Credit Authorization	Amount
City Cyclists (1)	
CR5241	($951.33)
CR6321	($1,484.68)
CR6592	($1,237.54)
CR6798	($727.56)
CR1608	($1,792.91)

c. In the Field Explorer, **select Formula Fields and click the New button.**

d. In the Name text box, **type *AbsCredit* and click OK.**

e. Expand the Functions tree, expand Math, and then double-click the Abs (x) function.

f. In the Report Fields tree, **expand the Credit table and double-click Amount.**

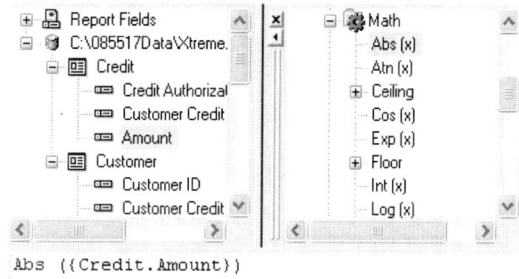

Abs ({Credit.Amount})

g. **Check the formula for errors and click OK.**

h. To return to the report, **click Save And Close.**

---

2. **Replace the Credit.Amount field with the AbsCredit field, formatting the label as needed.**

a. **Select the Design tab.**

b. From the Details section, **delete the Credit.Amount field.**

c. From the Field Explorer, **drag the AbsCredit formula field to where the Credit.Amount field was.**

d. In the Page Header section, **modify the AbsCredit field label so that it has a bottom border and a font size of 12, and reads** *Credits*

e. **Align the Credits field label with the Customer Name and Credit Authorization field labels.**

---

3. **Add a summary to the Group Footer #1 section that sums the AbsCredit field.**

   a. **Select the @AbsCredit field.**

   b. On the Insert Tools toolbar, **click the Insert Summary button** Σ.

   c. In the Calculate This Summary drop-down list, **verify that Sum is displayed.**

   d. From the Summary Location drop-down list, **select Group #1: Customer.Customer ID - A.**

   e. **Click OK.**

---

4. **Preview the report.**

   a. **Select the Preview tab.**

   b. **Observe the data displayed in the Credits column.** Notice that negative numbers are now displayed as absolute numbers.

Customer Name and Credit Authorization		Credits
City Cyclists (1)		
	CR5241	$951.33
	CR6321	$1,484.68
	CR6592	$1,237.54
	CR6798	$727.56
	CR1608	$1,792.91
		$6,194.02

   c. **Click the Show Next Page button.**

   d. **Observe the data for Spokes 'N Wheels Ltd.** Notice that it includes a null value because they have no credits.

   Spokes 'N Wheels Ltd. (8)

---

5. **Create a formula named *CreditSum* that replaces the sum of the AbsCredit field with "No Credits" when there is nothing in the field.**

   a. In the Field Explorer, **create a new formula named *CreditSum***

   b. In the Formula Text window, **type** `If IsNull`

c. Type **(Sum({@AbsCredit},⇒ {Customer.Customer ID}))** and press Enter.

```
If IsNull(Sum({@AbsCredit},{Customer.Customer ID}))
|
```

d. To return the text "No Credits" if the field is null, **type Then "No Credits"** and press Enter.

e. To return the credit amount and set the number of decimals to zero, **type Else ToText(Sum({@AbsCredit},⇒ {Customer.Customer ID}),0)**

```
If IsNull(Sum({@AbsCredit},{Customer.Customer ID}))
Then "No Credits"
Else ToText(Sum({@AbsCredit},{Customer.Customer ID}),0)
```

f. **Check the formula for errors and click OK.**

g. To return to the report, **click Save And Close.**

6. On the Design tab, **delete the Sum Of @AbsCredit field. Place CreditSum in the Group Header section.**

a. **Select the Design tab.**

b. From the Group Footer #1 section, **delete the Sum Of @AbsCredit field.**

c. In the Group Header #1 section, **insert the CreditSum field.**

PH	Customer Name and Credit Authorization	Credits
GH1	Group #1 Name	@CreditSum
D	Credit Authorization Number	@AbsCredit

7. Resize, bold, and align the @CreditSum field.

a. **Reduce the @CreditSum field width so that it is 1″ long.**

b. **Bold the @CreditSum field.**

c. On the Formatting toolbar, **click the Align Right button** [≣].

8. **Resize the Group Name field and preview the report.**

a. **Widen the Group #1 Name field so that it is 3″ long.**

b. **Select the Preview tab.**

c. **Observe the Order Total field.** Notice that the @CreditSum field for Spokes 'N Wheels Ltd. now displays "No Credits."

9. **Save and close the Customer Credit report.**

Lesson 4 Follow-up

In this lesson, you created formulas that allow you to display calculated data in your reports. Using formulas, you can enhance your reports by including information that may not be available in the associated database.

1. **What types of formulas will you create in your reports?**

2. **What types of parameter formulas will you create?**

LESSON 5
Formatting Reports

Lesson Time
45 minutes to 1 hour(s), 15 minutes

Lesson Objectives:

In this lesson, you will format reports.

You will:

- Remove white space from a report.
- Insert page header/footer data in a report.
- Add borders and lines to a report.
- Change the background color of a field.
- Change the margins of a report.

LESSON 5

Introduction

After creating a report and specifying the data you want to display, you may want to format the report to present the data a certain way. In this lesson, you will modify and format several layout elements.

By changing the way that a report looks, you can enhance a viewer's ability to identify and distinguish the report data. This can help to ensure that the data is received and interpreted the way that you intended.

TOPIC A

Remove White Space

Depending upon the amount of data in a report, there might be unnecessary and unwanted white space. In this topic, you will adjust section borders to remove excess white space.

You have created a report that contains some extra space within a section. By removing the extra white space, you will enhance the appearance of the report. In addition, you can decrease the number of pages in the report, saving scrolling time and paper when you print.

How to Remove White Space

Procedure Reference: Remove White Space

The amount of white space displayed between report rows is affected by the height of a section in relation to the objects within it. To remove white space from a report:

> 🖉 You can adjust a section on the Preview tab, but it is easier to do so in Design view, since visible lines appear between the sections in Design view.

1. If necessary, display the Design tab.

2. Remove the white space from the desired section.
   - Place the mouse pointer over the appropriate section's lower border and drag upward to decrease the white space. Note that you can only resize a section to the point of an existing field or vertical guideline.
   - Right-click the gray area of the desired section and choose Fit Section.
   - Or, suppress the section using the Section Expert dialog box.

3. If desired, preview the report.

ACTIVITY 5-1

Removing White Space

Data Files:

- Order Totals By Customer.rpt

Setup:

No files are open in Crystal Reports. The Start Page is displayed.

Scenario:

You inherited a report named Order Totals By Customer from another department. As soon as you open the report, you realize that there is too much white space in the Group Header #1 section.

What You Do	How You Do It
1. Identify how many pages are in the Order Totals By Customer report.	a. Open the Order Totals By Customer.rpt report.
	b. On the Preview tab, in the navigation buttons, **click the Show Last Page button.**
	c. **Observe the Auto Hide area.** Notice that the report has approximately 62 pages.
2. Remove the white space.	a. **Select the Design tab.**
	b. **Place the mouse pointer over the bottom Group Header #1 section boundary until a double-headed arrow is displayed.**
	c. **Drag the lower border up to the bottom of the Group #1 Name field.**

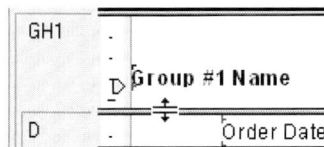

3. What happens when you try to move the section boundary up more?

Why can't the section's white space be further decreased?

---

4. Modify the section contents to remove more white space and preview the report.

a. Drag the Group #1 Name field to the top of the Group Header #1 section.

b. To remove the guide from the vertical ruler, **drag the guide to the left.**

GH1	.	Group #1 Name
D	.	Order Date

c. So that none of the characters are cut off, **increase the height of the Group #1 Name field.**

d. **Drag the section's lower border up to the edge of the Group #1 Name field.**

GH1	.	Group #1 Name
D	.	Order Date

e. **Select the Preview tab.**

f. **Observe the Auto Hide area.** Notice that the report now has fewer pages.

TOPIC B

Insert Page Header/Footer Data

In addition to modifying white space in your reports, there are many other formatting options you can apply. One of those options includes adding data to the top and bottom of each page. In this topic, you will add fields to Page Header and Page Footer sections.

Using a page header and footer enables you to add information to a report once so that information will be repeated on each page in the desired location.

How to Insert Page Header/Footer Data

Procedure Reference: Insert Page Header/Footer Data

To add data to Page Header and Page Footer sections:

1. If necessary, display the Design tab.

2. Using the Standard toolbar or the Field Explorer, drag the field(s) or other content to be added to the Page Header and/or Page Footer section(s).

   > Using the Page N Of M field may slow the performance of Crystal Reports because Crystal Reports must first format all pages to supply the total page count.

3. If desired, format the fields and other content.

4. If desired, preview the report.

Special Fields

In addition to adding database fields, formula fields, and parameter fields to your reports, there are other types of fields you can add, including special fields. *Special fields* are system-generated fields, such as Page Number, Print Date, File Path And Name, and Report Comments that can be added to any section in a report, such as the Page Header and Page Footer sections, to provide information about that report.

ACTIVITY 5-2

Inserting Page Header/Footer Data

Setup:

The Order Totals By Customer.rpt report and the Field Explorer are displayed on the Preview tab.

Scenario:

You need the Order Totals By Customer report to show a page number reference. Also, this report will be located in a folder separate from most other reports, so you need to display the path and file name at the bottom of each page.

What You Do	How You Do It
1. Place the page number data on the right side of the Page Header section.	a. Select the **Design** tab.
	b. In the Field Explorer, **expand the Special Fields category.**
	c. At the top of the Page Header section, **drag the Page N Of M field to the 4″ mark.**
2. Resize the Page N Of M field and preview the report.	a. Using the right sizing handle, **resize the Page N Of M field to about 1″.**
	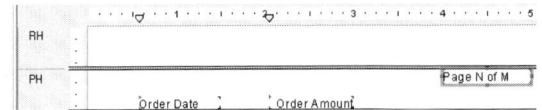
	b. Select the **Preview** tab.
	c. **Observe the Page Header section.** Notice that the special field is displayed.
3. Place the Page Footer data.	a. Select the **Design** tab.

b. From the Field Explorer's Special Fields category, **drag the File Path And Name field to the top left of the Page Footer section.**

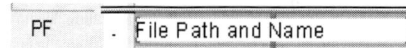

```
PF        . │File Path and Name      │
```

---

4. **Format the Page Footer data.**

a. **Widen the File Path And Name field so that it extends to the 4″ mark.**

b. From the Font Size drop-down list, **select 8.**

c. **Select the Preview tab.**

d. In the navigation buttons, **click the Show First Page button.**

e. **Scroll to the bottom of the first page.**

f. **Observe the Page Footer.** Notice that the file's path and name are displayed.

Athens Bicycle Co. (175.00)
```
│C:\085517Data\Order Totals By Customer.rpt│
```

TOPIC C

Add Borders, Boxes, and Lines

You have added a page header and page footer to your report. There are many other formatting changes that you might want to make to your report. In this topic, you will apply some more formatting by adding borders and lines.

Adding borders, boxes, and lines to a report increases the usefulness of your report by emphasizing important data. Also, your report will be more visually pleasing.

Borders, Boxes, and Lines

The purpose of borders, boxes, and lines is to increase the usefulness of your report by emphasizing important data. A *border* is a visible representation of a field or other text object's boundaries. You can add a border to the top, bottom, right, or left edge of a field or other object, or to any combination of the object's edges. Boxes and lines are freeform objects that can be drawn and positioned independently of other layout items.

Unlike fields and text objects, lines and boxes can span multiple report sections.

How to Add Borders, Boxes, and Lines

Procedure Reference: Display Borders

To display borders around report fields or labels:

Formatting changes can be made on either the Design tab or the Preview tab.

1. If necessary, display the desired tab.

2. Select the object whose border you want to display.

3. Display the object's Format Editor dialog box and select the Border tab.

4. Set the appropriate border options. You can change the line style, color, and background color of a border.

   A preview of what the border settings will look like is displayed at the bottom of the tab in the Sample area.

5. Click OK to apply the settings.

   To quickly add or remove a border, select the desired border option from the Borders drop-down list on the Formatting toolbar.

Procedure Reference: Add Lines

To add freeform lines to a report:

✎ You can only draw horizontal and vertical lines.

1. Change the mouse pointer to a pencil.
   - On the Insert Tools toolbar, click the Insert Line button.
   - Or, choose Insert→Line.

2. Place the mouse pointer where you want to begin the line.

3. Drag to the desired length and release the mouse button.

Procedure Reference: Add Boxes

To add boxes to a report:

1. Change the mouse pointer to a pencil.
   - On the Insert Tools toolbar, click the Insert Box button.
   - Or, choose Insert→Box.

2. Place the mouse pointer where you want to begin the box.

3. Drag diagonally to establish the box's height and width.

ACTIVITY 5-3

Adding Borders and Lines

Setup:

The bottom of the first page of the Order Totals By Customer.rpt report is displayed on the Preview tab.

Scenario:

After reviewing the Order Totals By Customer report, you notice that the group totals blend with the surrounding data. You need to format the field so that data stands out.

What You Do	How You Do It
1. Add a border to the Sum Of Orders.Order Amount field.	a. Select the Design tab.
	b. In the Group Footer #1 section, **right-click the Sum Of Orders.Order Amount field and choose Format Field.**
	c. In the Format Editor dialog box, **select the Border tab.**

d. Under Line Style, from the Left drop-down list, **select Double.**

Line style:
Left: Double

e. **Change the Right, Top, and Bottom line styles to Double.**

f. Under Color, from the Border drop-down list, **select Teal.**

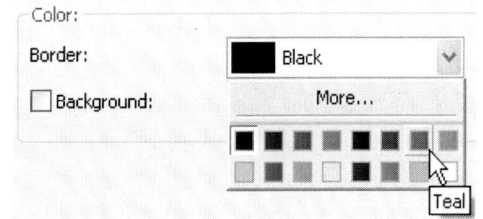

Color:
Border: Black
☐ Background: More...

Teal

g. **Click OK.**

2. **Draw a line to separate each data grouping in the report.**

a. To increase the height of the Group Footer #1 section, **drag the lower border down about one-eighth inch.**

b. On the Insert Tools toolbar, **click the Insert Line button** .

c. Beginning at the left margin of the Group Footer #1 section, below the Sum Of Orders.Order Amount field, **drag to the right to the 7.5″ mark.**

3. **Preview the report.**

a. **Select the Preview tab.**

b. **Scroll to the top of page 1.**

c. **Observe the Orders.Order Amount fields and group footers.** Each one of the formatted fields now displays a teal double border and each group is separated by a line.

Order Date   Order Amount
7 Bikes For 7 Brothers (132.00)
05/26/2004 $53.90
                              $53.90

TOPIC D

Change Field Background Color

You have added a colored border and a line to the report. There are many other ways that you can add color to your reports. In this topic, you will change the background color of a field.

Changing the background color of a field increases the usefulness of your report by highlighting the specified data. The user will immediately be drawn to the data with the highlighted background, and will be able to easily distinguish that data from the surrounding data.

How to Change Field Background Color

Procedure Reference: Change a Field's Background Color

To change the background color of a field:

1. If necessary, display the desired tab.

2. Select the object whose background you want to display.

3. Display the object's Format Editor dialog box and select the Border tab.

4. Under Color, check the Background check box to enable the Background drop-down list.

5. From the Background drop-down list, select the background color of your choice.

6. Click OK to apply the settings.

ACTIVITY 5-4

Changing a Field's Background Color

Setup:

The bottom of the first page of the Order Totals By Customer.rpt report is displayed on the Preview tab.

Scenario:

After reviewing the report, you need to use a colored background, rather than a border, to emphasize the totals.

What You Do	How You Do It
1. Remove the border from the Sum Of Orders.Order Amount field.	a. With the Preview tab still displayed, select the Sum Of Orders.Order Amount field for 7 Bikes For 7 Brothers.

7 Bikes For 7 Brothers (132.00)

05/26/2004 $53.90

$53.90

| | b. On the Formatting toolbar, display the Border button's drop-down list and select the No Border button. |

2. **Change the background color of the Sum Of Orders.Order Amount field.**

a. With the Sum Of Orders.Order Amount field still selected, **choose Format→ Format Field.**

b. **Select the Border tab.**

c. Under Color, **check the Background check box.**

d. From the Background drop-down list, **select Yellow.**

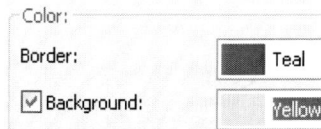

e. **Click OK.**

f. **Deselect the Sum Of Orders.Order Amount field.**

g. **Observe the Sum Of Orders.Order Amount field's background.** The double border has been removed and the field now has a yellow background that simulates highlighting.

7 Bikes For 7 Brothers (132.00)
05/26/2004 $53.90
                   $53.90

---

3. **Save and close the Order Totals By Customer report.**

TOPIC E

Change the Margins

You have formatted the contents that appear within a report. You can also modify the formatting of a report itself. In this topic, you will modify a report's margins.

Changing a report's margins can increase or reduce the amount of vertical white space available between columns. Margin settings can also be used to control the amount of data to be displayed on a page. Lastly, modifying a report's margins can accommodate a narrower or wider margin for different binding processes.

How to Change the Margins

Procedure Reference: Change Margins

To change the margins in a report:

1. Display the Page Setup dialog box.
   - Choose File→Page Setup.
   - Or, right-click in a blank area of the report and choose Page Setup.

2. Under Margins, change the Left, Top, Right, and Bottom margins as desired.

3. Click OK to apply the settings.

ACTIVITY 5-5

Changing Margins

Data Files:

- Employee Guide.rpt

Setup:

No files are open in Crystal Reports. The Start Page is displayed.

Scenario:

The Employee Guide report is going to be bound and distributed to all employees in the company; however, with the current formatting, there isn't enough space for the binding.

What You Do	How You Do It
1. Preview the Employee Guide report.	a. Open the Employee Guide.rpt report.
	b. On the Standard toolbar, **click the Print Preview button.**

c. **Observe the left margin.** It is set to 0.25".

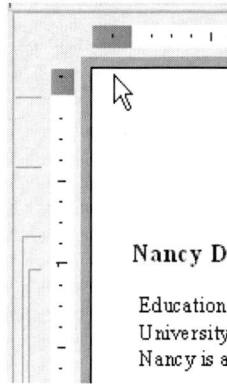

---

2. **Make the left margin 1".**

a. **Choose File→Page Setup.**

b. **Double-click in the Left margin text box.**

c. **Type** *1*

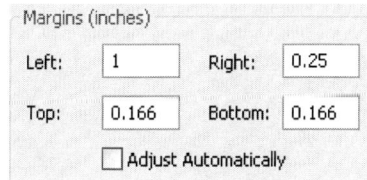

d. **Click OK.**

e. **Observe the left margin.** It is now set to 1" and can accommodate the binding process.

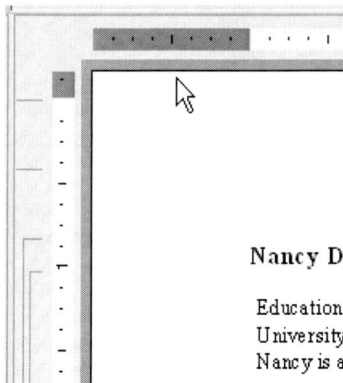

---

3. Save and close the Employee Guide report.

Lesson 5 Follow-up

In this lesson, you worked with a number of options for formatting your reports. By changing the way that a report looks, you can create reports that are easy to read and analyze.

1. What types of information will you place in the Page Header and Page Footer sections of your reports?

2. In what instances would you use borders, boxes, and lines to enhance your reports?

LESSON 6
Enhancing Reports

Lesson Time
1 hour(s) to 1 hour(s),
30 minutes

Lesson Objectives:

In this lesson, you will add and modify elements in a report.

You will:

- Add a watermark to a report.
- Add the contents of another file to a report using OLE.
- Modify formatting based on the value of specific data.
- Conditionally suppress a report section.
- Insert a hyperlink into a report.
- Hide blank report sections.

Introduction

You have improved the appearance of a report by applying some formatting. There are other options that you can use to enhance your report. In this lesson, you will examine those options.

You can enhance your reports to make them more useful by adding options such as watermarks, conditional formatting, and hyperlinks.

TOPIC A

Add a Watermark

One way that you can enhance a report or indicate its status is to add a graphic to the report's background. In this topic, you will insert a watermark.

One of the most obvious ways to enhance or communicate the status of a report is to use a watermark. For example, adding a company logo to a report clearly identifies ownership of the report. Another instance of a watermark's effectiveness is adding a "Confidential" watermark to a report. Such a watermark clearly indicates that the report contains sensitive information.

Section Expert

The purpose of the Section Expert is to format and manage report sections. You can use the Section Expert to insert, delete, merge, rearrange, and suppress sections. The Section Expert can also control watermark positioning, as well as report page numbering and break options, determining how the content will be displayed and printed.

How to Add a Watermark

Procedure Reference: Add a Watermark

To create a watermark by underlaying it in a new section:

1. If necessary, insert a new section.
    a. On the Expert Tools toolbar, click the Section Expert button to display the Section Expert dialog box.
    b. In the Sections list, select the section after which you want to insert a new section.
    c. Click Insert to insert the new section below the selected section.
    d. Click OK to close the Section Expert dialog box.

    📌 To create a new section, you can also right-click in the gray area of the appropriate section in the report and choose Insert Section Below.

2. Insert the graphic you want to underlay as a watermark.
    a. On the Insert Tools toolbar, click the Insert Picture button. The Open dialog box is displayed.
    b. Select the graphic you want to insert.

c.   Click Open. An object frame is attached to the mouse pointer.

d.   Click to place the picture in the appropriate section.

📌 To insert a graphic, you can also choose Insert→Picture.

3.   Modify the section containing the watermark graphic so that the following sections overlay it.

a.   Display the Section Expert dialog box.

b.   In the Sections list, select the section containing the watermark graphic.

c.   On the Common tab, check the Underlay Following Sections check box and click OK.

Page Break Insertion Options

Besides adding new sections, there are other options you can set when using the Section Expert dialog box. You want to control the page breaks in your report. The options that you can use in the Section Expert that allow you to do that are outlined in the following table.

Option	Function
New Page Before	Starts a new page before printing the selected section.
New Page After	Starts a new page after printing the selected section. Using the New Page After option on a group will insert a blank page at the end of your report (or display whatever is in your report footer on the last page). If this is not desired, a conditional format formula can be set on the New Page After option. The formula would read as follows: Not OnLastRecord.
Keep Together	Prevents a page break from being inserted in the middle of the selected section.

📌 The Keep Together option in the Section Expert dialog box is different than the Keep Groups Together option in the Insert Group and Change Group Options dialog boxes. The option in the Section Expert works at the record level, while the group option works at the group level.

Reasons to Create Sections

Crystal Reports provides five default sections in every report. Those sections are the Report Header, Report Footer, Page Header, Page Footer, and Details. If necessary, you can create additional sections. By doing so, you will have more control over report formatting.

Reason for Creating an Additional Section	Example
Avoid overlapping objects such as text fields with the Can Grow option, charts, and subreports	A chart grows as data expands, covering up the data below the chart. Putting the chart in its own section solves the problem.
Conditional formatting—suppress based on non-field criteria	Print company logo in Page Header A on every other page. Show Page Header B (with column labels) on each page.
Conditional formatting—suppress based on field value	Imagine two different format options for an invoice item: One format is for overdue accounts, done with bold fonts and account aging information. The other format is standard. If two Details sections are used, one can use conditional formatting to show the appropriate format desired based on the age of the invoice.
Show page labels in drill-down reports when reset formulas exist in the header sections	Page labels can be repeated at the top of drill-down reports. (Choose File→Report Options. Check the Show All Headers On Drill-Down check box.) Variable formulas often require a reset in the header sections, though, causing incorrect totals when headers are repeated in drill-down sections. One solution is to put page labels in Details A instead of the Page Header, checking Suppress If Duplicated on each field.
Widow/orphan control	Creating additional group sections is required for a detailed widow/orphan control.

ACTIVITY 6-1

Creating Watermarks

Data Files:

- Order Details.rpt
- Draft.bmp

Setup:

No files are open in Crystal Reports. The Start Page is displayed.

Scenario:

You created a report named Order Details. You need to distribute it to others for feedback. The report is in a draft stage, and you need to let the reviewers know it is a draft.

What You Do	How You Do It
1. In the Order Details report, **create a second Page Header section.**	a. **Open Order Details.rpt.**
	b. **Observe the Page Header section.** Notice that it contains the field labels.
	c. On the Expert Tools toolbar, **click the Section Expert button** 📑.
	d. In the Sections list, **select Page Header and click Insert.**

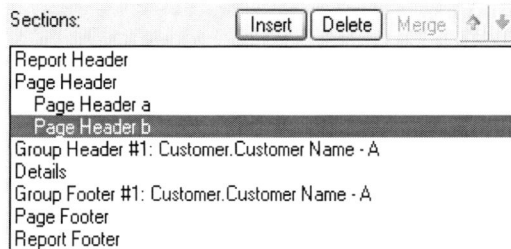

Sections: [Insert] [Delete] [Merge] ⬆ ⬇
```
Report Header
Page Header
   Page Header a
   Page Header b
Group Header #1: Customer.Customer Name - A
Details
Group Footer #1: Customer.Customer Name - A
Page Footer
Report Footer
```

	e. **Click OK.**

f. **Observe the Page Header sections.**
Notice that the original Page Header, now
Page Header A, has been separated from
the columns. Page Header B is blank.

---

2. **Insert the watermark graphic in the Page Header A section.**

a. In the gray area, **drag the Page Header A section below the Page Header B section.**

b. **Observe the Page Header names.** The two sections have switched positions, but the top section remains Page Header A, and the bottom one remains Page Header B.

c. On the Insert Tools toolbar, **click the Insert Picture button** .

d. In the C:\085517Data folder, **verify that Draft.bmp is selected and click Open.**

e. An object frame is attached to the mouse pointer (currently displayed as an hourglass).

f. In the Page Header A section, **place the mouse pointer at approximately the 1.5″ mark.**

g. **Click to place the picture in the Page Header A section.**

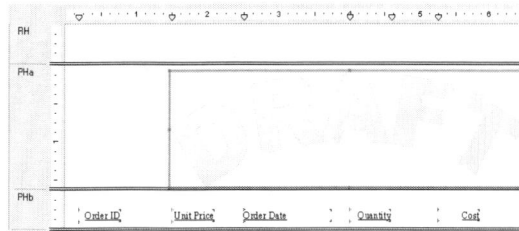

---

3. **Underlay the following sections and preview the report.**

a. On the Expert Tools toolbar, **click the Section Expert button.**

b. In the Sections list, **select Page Header A.**

c. On the Common tab, **check the Underlay Following Sections check box and click OK.**

d. **Click the Print Preview button.**

Order Date	Quantity	Cost
12/02/2003	1	$41.00
Subtotal:	1	
12/02/2003	3	$101.70
12/02/2003	3	$4,958.58
Subtotal:	6	

e. **Observe the watermark.** Notice that it underlays all the sections.

TOPIC B

Insert Objects Using Object Linking and Embedding

Watermarks are only one way to enhance a report. You can also add the contents of a file from another application. In this topic, you will add items from other applications using Object Linking and Embedding.

You have a report and you want to include some information from another application. You can simply choose to include a copy of the data or you can link to the external data. Linking means that any time the data is updated, in either Crystal Reports or in another program, the changes will be reflected in both locations.

Object Linking and Embedding

There are many types of objects that you can include in your reports. Object Linking and Embedding, also known as *OLE*, allows you to embed an object, such as a spreadsheet, text document, or video clip, into a document called the container application. When you double-click the object, the application in which the object was created, called the server application, is launched so you can edit it.

Linking Objects

If you want, you can link an object instead of embedding it. In this case, the container application does not physically hold the object, but provides a pointer to it. If you make a change to the linked object, all the documents that contain that same link are automatically updated the next time you open them.

How to Insert Objects Using Object Linking and Embedding

Procedure Reference: Insert Objects Using Object Linking and Embedding

To add an existing item to a report as an OLE object:

1. If necessary, select the Design tab.

2. Choose Insert→OLE Object. The Insert Object dialog box is displayed.

3. Select Create From File and click Browse. The Browse dialog box is displayed.

4. Select the file you want to insert and click Open to return to the Insert Object dialog box.

5. Specify whether or not to maintain a link between the placed object and the original file.
   - If you want modifications to the original file to be reflected in the report, check the Link check box.
   - If you want to be able to modify the object in the report without affecting the original file and vice versa, uncheck the Link check box.

6. Click OK to close the Insert Object dialog box.

7. Place the mouse pointer in the section in which you want to add the object and click to insert the OLE object.

8. If desired, double-click the OLE object to modify it.

ACTIVITY 6-2

Adding an OLE Item to a Report

Setup:

Microsoft Word has been installed following the setup instructions. The Order Details.rpt report is displayed on the Preview tab.

Scenario:

You received a Word document containing a bulleted list of items from a meeting. You would like to include that list in your report, and need to be able to modify the placed version without impacting the original file, and vice versa.

What You Do	How You Do It
1. Add the Action Items.doc file as an OLE object in the Report Header at the first guideline.	a. Select the Design tab and choose Insert→OLE Object.
	b. Select the Create From File option.
	c. Click Browse.
	d. In the C:\085517Data folder, select Action Items.doc and click Open.

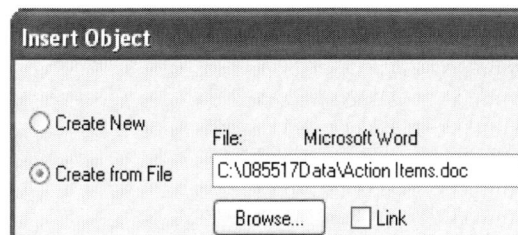

Insert Object

○ Create New   File: Microsoft Word
◉ Create from File   C:\085517Data\Action Items.doc
   Browse...   ☐ Link

e. Because you don't want any changes to impact the original file, **verify that the Link check box is unchecked.**

f. **Click OK.**

> It will take a moment for the object frame to display.

g. In the Report Header section, **place the mouse pointer at the 1/8″ mark on the ruler.**

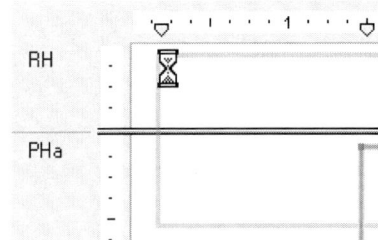

h. To place the OLE object in the Report Header section, **click at the 1/8″ mark on the ruler.**

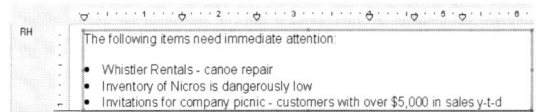

2. You realize that the first action item has been resolved. **Remove the first item from the list.**

a. To display the tooltip, **place the mouse pointer over the inserted object.**

b. **Observe the tooltip.** The tooltip indicates that the bulleted list is an OLE object.

c. **Double-click the OLE object.**

d. Microsoft Word menus and toolbars are now displayed along with those of Crystal Reports. **Select the first bulleted item.**

e. **Press Delete.**

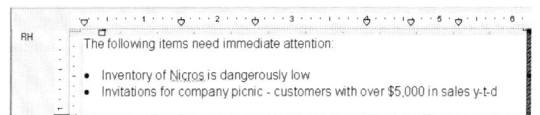

f. To deselect the object, **click within a blank area of the report.**

3. **Preview the report.**

a. **Select the Preview tab.**

b. **Observe the OLE object.** Notice that it is displayed in the Report Header section.

4. Save and close the Order Details report.

TOPIC C

Modify Formatting Based on Data Value

Another way you can enhance a report is to specify the look of particular report data based on the data's value. In this topic, you will use the Highlighting Expert to emphasize data based on criteria you select.

You are creating a report listing the sales generated by your sales staff. You want to emphasize those on the staff who have met or exceeded the monthly sales goal; you could do so using the Highlighting Expert dialog box.

Highlighting Expert

The purpose of the Highlighting Expert is to apply conditional formatting to report data based on criteria you specify. The formatting applied depends upon the selected field's value or upon that of another field's value. The Highlighting Expert enables you to control more than simple background highlighting. It provides control over all aspects of a field's formatting, from font style and color to border styles.

How to Modify Formatting Based on Data Value

Procedure Reference: Modify Formatting Based on Data Value

To highlight text based on criteria you specify:

1. Select the field you want to affect.

2. Display the Highlighting Expert dialog box.
   - On the Expert Tools toolbar, click the Highlighting button.
   - Choose Format→Highlighting Expert.
   - Or, right-click the desired field and choose Highlighting Expert.

3. Under Item List, click New.

4. Under Item Editor, from the Value Of drop-down list, select the field that will be affected.

5. From the second drop-down list, select the appropriate comparison operator.

6. In the third drop-down list, type the appropriate value.

7. Modify the Font Style, Font Color, Background, and Border options as desired.

8. Click OK.

9. If desired, preview the report to see the Highlighting Expert's results.

ACTIVITY 6-3

Modifying Format Based on Data Value

Data Files:

- Orders.rpt

Setup:

No files are open in Crystal Reports. The Start Page is displayed.

Scenario:

Customers with orders that are $5,000 or greater are members of the Platinum Club. You need their orders to stand out from the others so that they are immediately identifiable as members of the Platinum Club.

What You Do	How You Do It
1. Display the Highlighting Expert for the Order Amount field.	a. Open Orders.rpt.
	b. Select the Design tab and select the Order Amount field in the Details section.
	c. On the Expert Tools toolbar, **click the Highlighting button** 🔃.
2. Set the item to be greater than or equal to 5,000.	a. Under Item List, **click New.**
	b. Under Item Editor, **verify that the Value Of drop-down list displays This Field.**
	c. From the second Value Of drop-down list, **select Is Greater Than Or Equal To.**
	d. In the third drop-down list, **click and type** *5000*

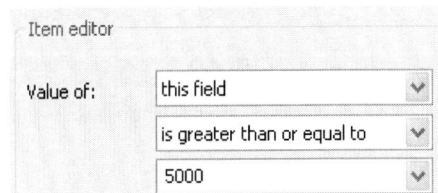

Item editor

Value of:	this field	⌄
	is greater than or equal to	⌄
	5000	⌄

3. **Specify formatting for the fields that meet the criteria.**

   a. From the Font Style drop-down list, **select Bold.**

   b. From the Font Color drop-down list, **select Blue.**

   c. From the Background drop-down list, **select Silver.**

Font style:	Bold
Font color:	■ Blue
Background:	☐ Silver
Border:	Default border style
Sample:	($55,555.56)

   d. **Click OK.**

   e. To deselect the Order Amount field, **click in a blank area of the report.**

4. **Preview the report.**

   a. **Select the Preview tab.**

   b. To hide the Group Tree, on the Standard toolbar, **click the Toggle Group Tree button** .

   c. **Observe the Order Amount column.** Notice that orders greater than or equal to $5,000 are highlighted.

5. **Save and close the Orders report.**

TOPIC D

Suppress Report Sections

Another way to make your report more effective is to hide report information based on specified criteria. In this topic, you will use a formula to suppress a section.

Your boss is thinking about closing the business for one day. He wants to check the sales that have occurred in the past on that day to see how a closing might affect the business. You can create a formula and suppress all sales except for those made on that day based on the formula. Therefore, only the sales you specify will be displayed, making it easier to focus on that data.

Attribute and Boolean Formatting

There are two types of formulas that accomplish conditional formatting: attribute and boolean.

Formula Type	Description
Attribute	An *attribute formula* requires additional information to specify the formatting properties. For example, font color is not something that is turned on or off. Rather, a color name must be provided, such as red, blue, gray, and so forth. Attribute formatting uses an If-Then-Else statement rather than a boolean formula. A sample attribute formatting example would be: If {Orders.Order Quantity} > 500 then crRed else crDefaultAttribute.
Boolean	A *boolean formula* is any formula that returns a true/false value. For example, a boolean formula might be used in a conditional format formula to indicate whether the formatting option in question should be turned on (true) or off (false).

How to Suppress Report Sections

Procedure Reference: Conditionally Suppress Report Sections

To conditionally suppress report sections:

1. Display the Section Expert dialog box.
   - On the Expert Tools toolbar, click the Section Expert button.
   - Choose Report→Section Expert.
   - Or, right-click in the gray area and choose Section Expert.

2. In the Sections list, select the section that includes the data you want to suppress.

3. On the Common tab, to the right of the Suppress (No Drill-Down) check box, click the Conditional Formula button. The Formula Workshop is displayed.

4. Create the necessary formula.

5. Check the formula for errors.

6. Click Save And Close to return to the Section Expert dialog box.

7. Click OK to apply the settings and close the Section Expert dialog box.

8. If desired, preview the report. Note that you could have created a selection formula limiting the report to Saturday and Sunday. However, the totals would only
include the filtered data. When the data is suppressed, totals in the report reflect
all records, including those that have been suppressed.

Procedure Reference: Conditionally Suppress Field Data

To conditionally suppress field data:

1. Select the field(s) to be suppressed.

2. Display the Format Editor dialog box.
   - On the Expert Tools toolbar, click the Format button.
   - Choose Format→Field.
   - Or, right-click the selected field(s) and choose Format Field.

3. On the Common tab, to the right of the Suppress check box, click the Conditional
   Formula button. The Formula Workshop is displayed.

4. Create the necessary formula.

5. Check the formula for errors.

6. Click Save And Close to return to the Format Editor dialog box.

7. Click OK to apply the settings and close the Format Editor dialog box.

8. If desired, preview the report.

DayOfWeek Function

Another function that you might want to use when creating formulas is DayOfWeek.
This function determines the day of the week that the given date falls on and converts
the day of the week to a number, 1 to 7. For example, DayOfWeek (Date(1990,10,1))
would return the number 2 because October 1, 1990 was a Monday. (Crystal Reports
uses Sunday as day 1, unless otherwise specified in the formula.)

ACTIVITY 6-4

Conditionally Suppressing a Report Section

Data Files:

- Weekend Orders.rpt

Setup:

No files are open in Crystal Reports. The Start Page is displayed.

Scenario:

You have created a report named Weekend Orders. The marketing department is conducting some research, and has requested a list of customers who ordered items on Saturdays and Sundays.

What You Do	How You Do It
1. Identify the number of items ordered during the first half of 2003.	a. Open Weekend Orders.rpt.
	b. Observe the Group Footer #1 section. Notice that it includes the Sum Of Orders_ Details.Quantity field to display the total number of orders placed during that period.
	c. On the Standard toolbar, **click the Print Preview button.**
	d. In the navigation buttons, **click the Show Next Page button and scroll down to locate the total number of orders.**
	e. Observe the Sum Of Orders_ Details.Quantity field. There were 163 items that were ordered in the first half of 2003.
2. Display the Format Formula Editor window for the Details section.	a. On the Expert Tools toolbar, **click the Section Expert button** 📲.
	b. In the Sections list, **select Details.**
	c. On the Common tab, to the right of the Suppress (No Drill-Down) check box, **click the Conditional Format button** ⊞.

3. The Format Formula Editor window is displayed in the Formula Workshop. **Create a conditional formula for the Details section that suppresses sales that did not occur on Saturday and Sunday.**

a. To determine the day of the week and convert it to a number, in the Formula Text window, **type DayOfWeek(**

b. Using the Report Fields tree, **add the Orders.Order Date field to the formula, then type) and press the Spacebar.**

c. To include the days of the week that follow Sunday, **type >1 and press the Spacebar.**

d. To include additional criteria, **type and**

e. **Press Enter.**

f. **Repeat steps a and b.**

g. To include the days of the week prior to Saturday, **type < 7**

```
DayOfWeek({Orders.Order Date}) >1 and
DayOfWeek({Orders.Order Date}) <7
```

🖈 You could copy and paste the first line of the formula and edit the components as appropriate.

4. **Verify that the formula is correct and return to the Section Expert dialog box.**

a. **Click the Check button.**

b. No errors are found. **Click OK.**

c. To return to the Section Expert dialog box, on the Formula Workshop's Save toolbar, **click Save And Close.**

d. **Observe the Conditional Formula button for the Suppress (No Drill-Down) check box.** Notice that the icon on the button has changed indicating that a formula has been created.

e. **Click OK.**

5. **Preview the weekend orders placed in the first half of 2003.**

a. In the navigation buttons, **click the Show First Page button.**

Order Date	Product ID	Quantity
January 2003		
Sat 02/22/03	1107	1
Sat 02/22/03	2212	3
Sat 02/22/03	103151	2
Sat 02/22/03	101201	3
Sat 02/22/03	302222	2
Sat 02/22/03	2203	2
Sat 02/22/03	3305	3
Sat 02/22/03	2209	2
Sat 02/22/03	302221	2
Sat 02/22/03	1101	2
Sat 02/22/03	102201	3
Sat 02/22/03	2215	1
Sat 02/22/03	301151	2
Sat 02/22/03	302201	2
Sat 02/22/03	1107	1
		163

b. **Observe the data in the Order Date column.** Only weekend orders are displayed.

c. **Observe the Sum Of Orders_ Details.Quantity field.** The number of orders placed for the first half of 2003 remain at 163 because, when data is suppressed, report totals still reflect all records, including those suppressed.

TOPIC E

Insert Hyperlinks

You may want to provide your report users with supplemental or supporting information. You can do that by providing them with a method to display information outside the report. In this topic, you will add hyperlinks to a report.

You have some supporting data that you want to provide with a report. However, the report is too large and has limited white space, so it would be difficult to actually display the data in the report. By inserting a hyperlink, you can direct users to that additional information.

Hyperlinks

The purpose of a hyperlink is to provide users with a way to navigate from one location to another, whether that location is inside or outside of a report. A hyperlink can be displayed as either text or an icon. In Crystal Reports, you can insert a hyperlink to:

- A website
- A file
- A field value
- An email address
- Another Crystal Reports file

Access to Linked Information

Hyperlinks are saved in the report and are available to other users as a way of viewing additional information. However, the linked information is available only if the user has access to the location where the information is stored and the application necessary to display the information.

How to Insert Hyperlinks

Procedure Reference: Add a Hyperlink to a Report

To insert a hyperlink into a report:

1. If you do not already have an object that you want to use as a hyperlink, add a graphic or text object to the report.

2. If desired, format the new object.

3. Select the report object that you want to use as a hyperlink.

4. Display the Hyperlink tab in the Format Editor.
   - On the Expert Tools toolbar, click the Format button and select the Hyperlink tab.
   - On the Expert Tools toolbar, click the Insert Hyperlink button.
   - Or, choose Format→Hyperlink.

5. In the Hyperlink Type box, select the type of hyperlink you want to create.

6. In the Hyperlink Information box, type the appropriate information based on the hyperlink type.

7. Click OK to insert the hyperlink in the report.

ACTIVITY 6-5

Inserting Hyperlinks

Setup:
The first page of Weekend Orders.rpt is displayed on the Preview tab.

Scenario:
Although there is not enough room in the report, you need to provide users with a list of all customers.

What You Do	How You Do It
1. Add a text object to the left side of the Report Footer section to act as the hyperlink.	a. Select the Design tab.
	b. Click the Insert Text Object button **ab**.
	c. In the Report Footer section, **click in the left side to place the text object.**
	d. In the selected text object, **type** *View All Customer Orders: Microsoft Word Format*
	e. **Deselect the text object and widen it to 3.50".**

GF1	.		1.Quantity
RF	.	View All Customer Orders: Microsoft Word Format	

2. Format the text object so that it is blue and underlined.	a. With the text object still selected, on the Expert Tools toolbar, **click the Format button** 📑.
	b. **Select the Font tab.**
	c. From the Color drop-down list, **select Blue.**
	d. Under Effects, **check the Underline check box.**

3. **Create a hyperlink from the text object to the Customer Contacts.doc file.**

   a. With the Format Editor dialog box still displayed, **select the Hyperlink tab.**

   b. Under Hyperlink Type, **select the A File option.**

   c. Below the File Name text box, **click Browse.**

   d. If necessary, **navigate to the C:\085517Data folder.**

   e. From the Files Of Type drop-down list, **select All Files.**

   f. With the contents of the C:\085517Data folder displayed, **double-click the Customer Contacts.doc file.**

   g. **Click OK and deselect the formatted text object.**

4. **Preview the report and test the hyperlink.**

   a. **Select the Preview tab.**

   b. **Click the Show Last Page button and, if necessary, scroll to the bottom of the page.**

c. **Place the mouse pointer over the hyperlink.**

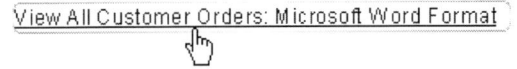

View All Customer Orders: Microsoft Word Format

d. **Observe the mouse pointer icon.** Notice that it changes from an arrow to a pointing hand.

e. **Click the hyperlink and, when prompted, click Yes.**

f. **Observe the displayed document.** The document displays customer names and phone numbers in Microsoft Word.

5. **Exit Word, save the Weekend Orders report, and close it.**

TOPIC F

Hide Blank Report Sections

You can further enhance a report by suppressing sections when they only contain fields that are blank. In this topic, you will suppress sections when the fields in those sections contain no data.

You have a report that displays salary information for all staff members in your department. Some staff member records display a bonus, along with a total compensation amount that totals the salary and bonus amounts. However, records for staff members who did not receive a bonus display two blank lines. You might want to suppress the blank lines.

Reasons for Hiding Report Objects

There are a number of reasons to hide report objects.

Reason to Hide Objects	Example
Duplex printing	Hide objects every other page.

Reason to Hide Objects	Example
Entire sections and/or fields can be hidden when the data is not applicable for a particular record	1. In an aging report, show only overdue accounts using conditional suppression. 2. Hide table headings when there is no data in the table. 3. Display the word "continued" only when in a repeated group header.
Formulas used for testing only	Suppressed objects display in Design mode. Keeping formulas used in testing provides quick report troubleshooting.
Formulas used for calculation purposes only	Running totals typically do not need to be shown in the Details section, but manual-running total formulas must be placed in each Details section to properly calculate.

How to Hide Blank Report Sections

Procedure Reference: Hide Blank Sections

To hide blank report sections or objects:

1. If necessary, distribute fields among several sections so that any field you may want to hide when blank is in its own section.

2. Display the Section Expert dialog box.
    *   On the Expert Tools toolbar, click the Section Expert button.
    *   Choose Report→Section Expert.
    *   Or, right-click in the gray area and choose Section Expert.

3. In the Sections list, select the section you want to suppress.

4. On the Common tab, check Suppress Blank Section.

5. Click OK to apply the setting and close the Section Expert dialog box.

Suppress vs. Suppress If Duplicated

Another option for suppressing sections is Suppress If Duplicated. If selected, Suppress If Duplicated prevents a field value from printing if it is duplicated within a report page. The value does not print, but the space in which it would have printed remains.

ACTIVITY 6-6

Hiding Report Sections

Data Files:

- Employee Addresses.rpt

Setup:

No files are open in Crystal Reports. The Start Page is displayed.

Scenario:

You have created a report named Employee Addresses. When you preview the report, you notice that some of the Address2 fields are blank, which negatively affects the appearance of the report.

What You Do	How You Do It
1. Preview the Employee Addresses report.	a. **Open Employee Addresses.rpt.**
	b. **Observe the Details section.** Notice that it includes an Address1 and an Address2 field.
	c. **Click the Print Preview button.**
	d. **Observe Nancy Davolio's information.** Notice that the Address2 field is blank.
	Nancy Davolio 507 - 20th Ave. E. Port Moody BC V3D 4F6 Employee_Addresses.Address2 (String)
2. Move the data you may want to suppress to its own section.	a. **Select the Design tab.**
	b. In the gray area of the Details section, **right-click and choose Insert Section Below.**

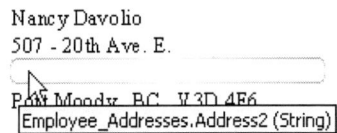

c. Add another new section below the original Details section.

d. Drag the @CityRegionZip field to the Details C section.

e. Drag the Address2 field to the Details B section.

f. To remove the excess space from the Details A section, using the Details C section's vertical sizing handle, **drag the section's lower border up approximately 1 inch.**

---

3. **Suppress the Details B section.**

a. On the Expert Tools toolbar, **click the Section Expert button.**

b. In the Sections list, **select Details B.**

c. On the Common tab, **check Suppress Blank Section.**

d. **Click OK.**

---

4. **Preview the Employee Addresses report.**

a. **Select the Preview tab.**

b. **Observe Nancy Davolio's information.** Notice that the Address2 field has been successfully suppressed.

Nancy Davolio
507 - 20th Ave. E.
Port Moody, BC   V 3D 4F6

5. **Save and close the Employee Addresses report.**

Lesson 6 Follow-up

In this lesson, you examined options for enhancing reports. By using such options as watermarks, conditional formatting, and hyperlinks, you will make your reports more useful.

1. **What type of conditional formatting might you use in your reports?**

2. **What types of report objects might you hide in your reports and why?**

LESSON 7
Creating Pie Charts

Lesson Time
*1 hour(s) to 1 hour(s),
30 minutes*

Lesson Objectives:

In this lesson, you will create single data series charts.

You will:

- Create a drill-down pie chart.
- Modify chart text.
- Format a pie chart.
- Create a grouped chart.

Introduction

You have worked with a number of different options that allow you to improve or enhance your reports. A graphical way to present data is to use charts. In this lesson, you will create and modify pie charts.

You have summarized data in a report. Graphic representations of data are often easier to understand. By using charts, you can present data graphically in a colorful, more meaningful way.

TOPIC A

Create a Pie Chart with a Drill-Down

Up to now you have represented data textually and numerically. However, you may want to create a graphical representation of that data. In this topic, you will create a pie chart.

If you have groups of data that you want to present graphically, using a pie chart, you can create a visually appealing report that represents data as percentages. For example, in a report displaying the first-quarter sales totals for each salesperson, you can display each person's sales as a percentage of total sales.

Chart Expert

You can create a new chart from that report data using the Chart Expert. The purpose of the Chart Expert is to guide you through the chart creation process while providing you with options for designing a chart.

Chart Types

When creating a chart in Crystal Reports, it is important to choose the chart type that best matches the data to be shown. See Table 7-1 for a description of the most common types.

Table 7-1: *Chart Types*

Type		Function
Bar		Compares several sets of data by using bars that are displayed side by side.
Line		Displays trends in data as a series of points connected by a line and is best suited for displaying data for a large number of groups.

Type	Function
Area	Displays data as areas that are filled with color or patterns, and is best suited for displaying data for a limited number of groups.
Pie	Displays data as percentages in a pie, split and filled with color or patterns and is usually used for one group of data.
Doughnut	Similar to a pie chart, it displays data as sections of a circle or doughnut, and can display the grand total in the hole in the middle.
3D Riser	Similar to a bar chart, it displays the extremes in your data in a series of three-dimensional objects, side by side, in a three-dimensional plane.
3D Surface	Displays a topographic view of multiple sets of data.
XY Scatter	Displays a group of plotted points that represent specific data in a pool of information, allowing the user to determine trends.
Radar	Displays group data at the perimeter of the radar and numeric values from the center of the radar to the perimeter, allowing the user to determine how specific group data relates to the whole of the group data.
Bubble	Similar to an XY Scatter chart, it displays data as a series of bubbles.
Stock	Displays high and low values for data and is useful for monitoring financial or sales activities.

Type		Function
Numeric Axis		A bar, line, or area chart that uses a numeric or date/time field as its On Change Of field.
Gauge		Displays values graphically as points on a gauge and is usually used for one group of data.
Gantt		A horizontal bar chart that provides a graphical illustration of a schedule. The horizontal axis displays a time span. The vertical axis displays a series of tasks or events.
Funnel		Similar to a pie chart or a stacked bar chart in that it displays data as percentages that add up to 100 percent, but it uses a funnel shape to display data percentages. Often used for pipeline analysis for sales forecasts.
Histogram		A type of bar chart that displays the frequency with which the data occurs.

Chart Layouts

In addition to chart type, you need to determine the layout of a chart. Crystal Reports provides you with four layouts from which to choose.

Layout	Function
Advanced	Use to graph multiple chart values and when there are no group or summary fields in a report. Can be placed in any section of a report, except Details.
Group	Use to graph data in summary fields. Must be placed in a summary section (Report Header, Report Footer, Group Header, or Group Footer).
Cross-Tab	Use to graph data in an existing cross-tab object, which is a grid that includes rows, columns, and summary fields.

Layout	Function
OLAP	Use to graph data in an existing OLAP (Online Analytical Processing) grid, which is used to display OLAP data. OLAP grid objects look and act much like cross-tab objects, but they are designed specifically for OLAP data.

Chart Elements

When you create a chart, it includes components that each have a specific function.

Chart Component	Function
Axis	A line that borders one side of the plot area in a chart, providing a reference for measuring or comparing data. The Y axis is usually vertical. The X axis is usually horizontal.
Data Points	Individual values in a chart.
Data Series	Related data points plotted collectively in a chart, represented by a marker.
Axes Labels	Text that provides additional information about a marker in relation to the axis scale.
Legend	A box that identifies the patterns or colors assigned to a data series.
Marker	A bar, area, plot, slice, or symbol that represents a data series in a chart.
Plot Area	An area within the axes of a chart that includes the data series.

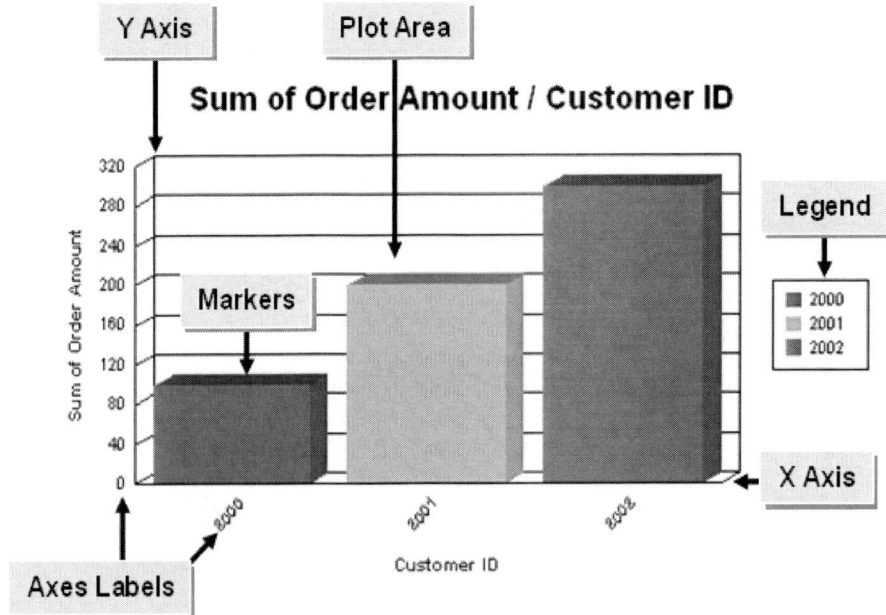

Figure 7-1: *This bar chart includes most chart components.*

Drill Down in a Chart

Much like a drill-down report only displays summarized data, you can create charts that do the same thing. For example, in a pie chart that includes a drill-down, you can allow users to view detailed information for each slice by double-clicking the slice.

Suppressed Regions

It is common to hide the detail when a report has a drill-down. When viewed in Design view, the hidden sections appear with gray diagonal lines, indicating that the data in those sections will be suppressed in Preview. If you right-click in the gray area of the Details section and choose Show, gray lines disappear, and the section data is no longer hidden.

Figure 7-2: *A suppressed section displays diagonal gray lines in Design view.*

How to Create a Pie Chart with a Drill-Down

Procedure Reference: Create a Pie Chart

To add a pie chart to a report:

1. Add a chart to the desired section.
    *   On the Insert Tools toolbar, click the Insert Chart button.
    *   Choose Insert→Chart.
    *   Or, right-click in the desired section and choose Insert Chart.

2. Click in the desired section to place the chart.

⚠ Depending upon the section in which you place the chart, the Chart Expert may not display automatically. If not, right-click the chart and choose Chart Expert.

3. On the Type tab, in the Choose Your Chart Type list, select Pie.

4. Select the Data tab.

5. Under Layout, select Group.

6. Under Data, from the On Change Of drop-down list, select the field on which you want to base the chart.

7. From the Show drop-down list, select the field you want to display in the chart.

8. If desired, select the Options tab and modify Chart Color, Data Points, Legend, and custom settings.

9. If desired, select the Color Highlight tab and apply conditional formatting to the chart by specifying conditions.

10. If desired, select the Text tab and add new titles or modify existing ones by changing their formatting.

11. Click OK to apply the settings to the chart. If you are viewing the chart on the Design tab, it may not display properly.

12. If desired, preview the chart on the Preview tab. Placing the mouse pointer over areas of the charted data will display the actual data in a tooltip.

ACTIVITY 7-1

Creating a Pie Chart with a Drill-Down

Data Files:

- Helmet Sales By Type.rpt

Setup:

No files are open in Crystal Reports. The Start Page is displayed.

Scenario:

You have a report named Helmet Sales By Type that displays helmet sales for a select group of customers. It is a very plain report, and the information may be difficult to interpret.

What You Do	How You Do It
1. Preview the Helmet Sales By Type report.	a. Open Helmet Sales By Type.rpt.

b. **Observe the Details A and Details B sections.** Notice that they contain gray diagonal lines, indicating that they are currently suppressed.

GH1	·	@Title		
Da	·	Order ID	Quantity	Product Name
Db	·	Order ID	Quantity	Product Name

---

2. **Create a pie chart based on the Product.Color field displaying the Sum Of Orders_Detail.Quantity data.**

a. On the Expert Tools toolbar, **click the Insert Chart button**.

b. To place the chart and display the Chart Expert, **click in the upper-left corner of the Report Header section.**

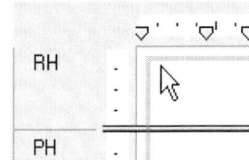

RH	·
	·
	·
PH	·

c. On the Type tab, in the Choose Your Chart Type list, **select Pie.**

d. **Select the Data tab.**

e. Under Layout, **select Group.**

f. Under Data, in the On Change Of drop-down list, **verify that Product.Color is selected.**

g. In the Show drop-down list, **verify that Sum Of Orders_Detail.Quantity is selected.**

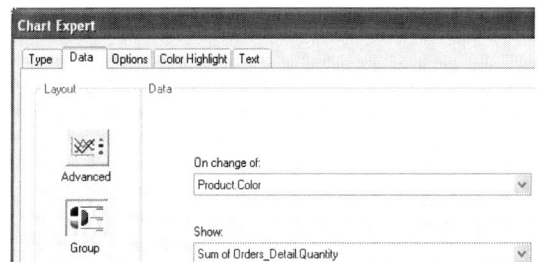

Chart Expert

Type | Data | Options | Color Highlight | Text

Layout

Advanced

Group

Data

On change of:
Product.Color

Show:
Sum of Orders_Detail.Quantity

h. **Click OK.**

Sum of Quantity / Color

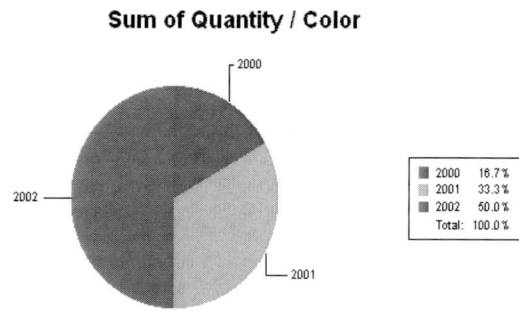

■	2000	16.7%
■	2001	33.3%
■	2002	50.0%
	Total:	100.0%

i. **Observe the chart.** Notice that the chart displays quantity by year rather than by color.

3. **Preview the report.**

a. With the chart selected, **click the Print Preview button.**

Sum of Quantity / Color

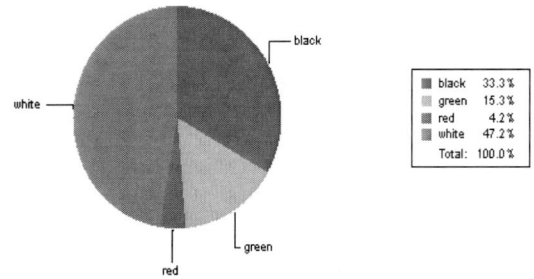

■ black	33.3%	
□ green	15.3%	
■ red	4.2%	
▨ white	47.2%	
Total:	100.0%	

b. **Observe the chart.** Notice that on the Preview tab the chart correctly displays quantity by color.

c. **Click the chart** to select it.

d. **Place the mouse pointer over the slice labeled Green.** The mouse pointer changes to a magnifying glass, indicating that the chart is a drill-down. **Observe the tooltip.** Notice that it displays the underlaying details for that slice of the pie.

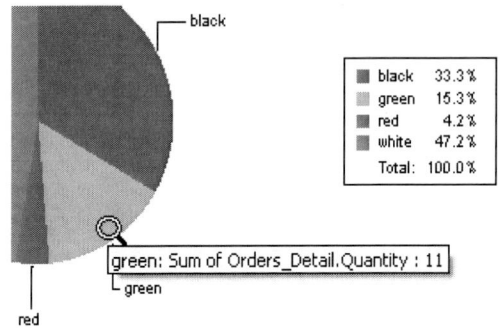

■ black	33.3%	
□ green	15.3%	
■ red	4.2%	
▨ white	47.2%	
Total:	100.0%	

green: Sum of Orders_Detail.Quantity : 11

TOPIC B

Modify Chart Text

Once you have created a chart, there are many ways you can modify it. In this topic, you will modify chart text.

You created a chart using the Chart Expert. After previewing it, you realize that the automatically generated chart title is not what you wanted, and the chart labels are too small to read comfortably. The ability to modify chart text allows you to ensure that the chart text is descriptive enough to represent the data.

How to Modify Chart Text

Procedure Reference: Modify Chart Text

To modify chart text:

1. Right-click the chart and choose Chart Expert.

2. Select the Text tab.

3. Modify the text as desired.

    - To customize the chart title, subtitle, or footnote, next to the appropriate option, uncheck the Auto-Text check box, and type the new title in the corresponding text box.

    - To change chart title, subtitle, footnote, or legend text font formatting, in the Font section, select the chart item you want to format, click Font, specify formatting options, and click OK.

4. Click OK to apply the changes to the chart text.

> 🔖 You can also choose Chart→Chart Options→Selected Item to access the Formatting dialog box for a selected chart item.

Procedure Reference: Modify Selected Chart Labels

To modify the font for the selected chart label:

1. Right-click the label, and from the shortcut menu, choose Format Data Label.

2. In the Format Data Labels dialog box, format the label as desired.

3. Click OK. Other labels of the same type will reflect the change as well.

Procedure Reference: Modify the Display of Legend Values

To modify the display of legend values:

1. Choose Chart→Chart Options and select the Legend tab.

2. Check the Show Values check box, and if desired, uncheck the Show Percents check box.

3. Click OK.

ACTIVITY 7-2

Modifying the Chart Text

Objective:
Change the chart text.

Setup:
The Helmet Sales By Type.rpt report is displayed on the Preview tab.

Scenario:
You need to change the chart title so that it better identifies the data in the chart. You also need to make the labels and legend text easier to read.

What You Do	How You Do It
1. Change the default chart title to *Quantity by Helmet Color*.	a. Right-click the chart and choose Chart Expert.
	b. Select the Text tab.
	c. Under Titles, to the right of Title, uncheck the Auto-Text check box.
	d. In the Title box, change the default text by typing *Quantity by Helmet Color*

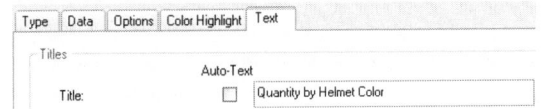

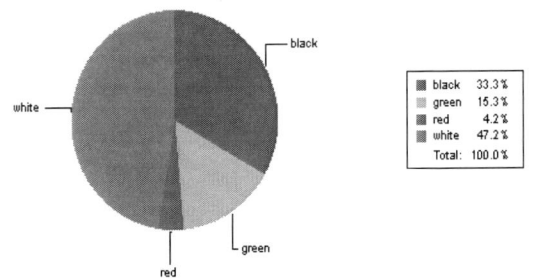

e. Click OK.

Quantity by Helmet Color

2. Increase the legend text to 10.

a. Display the Chart Expert and select the Text tab.

b. Under Format, in the list, **select Legend Title and click Font.**

c. In the Font dialog box, in the Size list box, **select 10 and click OK.**

d. To close the Chart Expert, **click OK.**

Quantity by Helmet Color

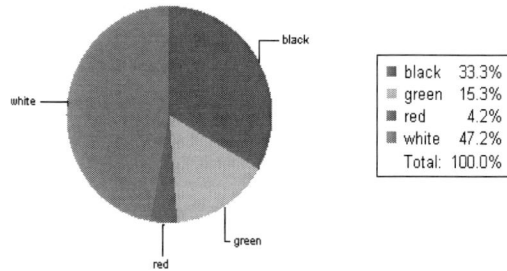

■ black	33.3%
■ green	15.3%
■ red	4.2%
■ white	47.2%
Total:	100.0%

3. Set the pie slice label size.

a. **Select the White pie slice label.**

b. **Right-click the selected label and choose Format Data Label.**

c. In the Format Data Labels dialog box, from the Size drop-down list, **select 10.**

Color: Size:

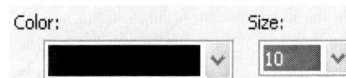

d. **Click OK.**

Quantity by Helmet Color

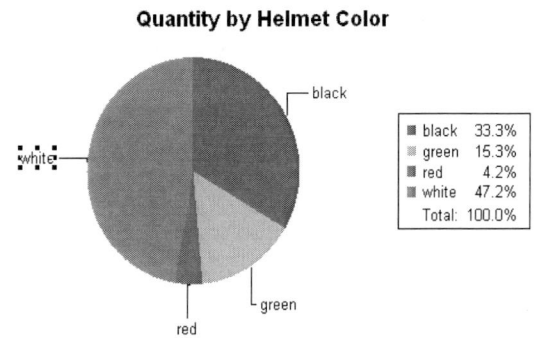

■ black	33.3%
▨ green	15.3%
■ red	4.2%
■ white	47.2%
Total:	100.0%

Topic C

Format a Chart

After you have created a chart and modified the chart text, you may want to also modify the appearance of other chart elements. In this topic, you will format a chart.

Once you create a chart, there are many formatting changes you can make to it, including changing the chart type and the display status. Being able to modify a chart's appearance enables you to present the data in the most useful and appealing manner possible.

How to Format a Chart

Procedure Reference: Change a Pie Chart's Layout

To change a pie chart's layout:

1. Right-click the chart and choose Chart Expert.

2. On the Type tab, in the Choose Your Chart Type list, select Doughnut.

3. If desired, to display the pie chart as a 3D chart, check the Use Depth Effect check box and click OK.

Procedure Reference: Modify Pie Slice and Border Colors

To change the color of individual pie chart slices:

1. Select the slice that you want a different color.

2. Display the Format Pie Slice dialog box.
   - Right-click the slice and choose Format Pie Slice.
   - Or, choose Chart→Format Pie Slice.

3. On the Fill tab, from the Foreground Color drop-down list, select the new color.

4. If desired, set Pattern, Gradient, Texture, and Picture options.

5. If desired, select the Border tab and set the Color, Style, and Thickness border options.

6. To apply the new settings, click OK.

Procedure Reference: Hide Data Labels and the Chart Legend

To hide data labels and the chart legend:

1. Choose Chart→Chart Options.

2. Select the Data Labels tab.

3. Uncheck the Show Labels check box.

4. If desired, uncheck the Show Pie Total check box.

5. Select the Legend tab.

6. Uncheck the Show Legend check box and click OK.

Procedure Reference: Resize and Reposition Chart Items

To resize and reposition chart elements:

1. Click the item you want to change so that selection handles appear around it.

2. Modify the item's size and position as desired.
   - To resize the selected object, place the mouse pointer over a selection handle and drag to the desired size.
   - To reposition the selected object, place the mouse pointer within the selected object's borders and drag the object to the desired position.

ACTIVITY 7-3

Formatting a Chart

Setup:

The Helmet Sales By Type.rpt report is displayed on the Preview tab.

Scenario:

At the client's request, you need to change the pie to a doughnut chart. In addition, the slice colors do not match the associated labels. You need to fix them so they match.

LESSON 7

What You Do	How You Do It
1. Change the pie chart to a ring pie chart.	a. Deselect the label.
	b. Right-click the chart and choose Chart Expert.
	c. On the Type tab, in the Choose Your Chart Type list, **select Doughnut.**
	d. **Click OK.**

Quantity by Helmet Color

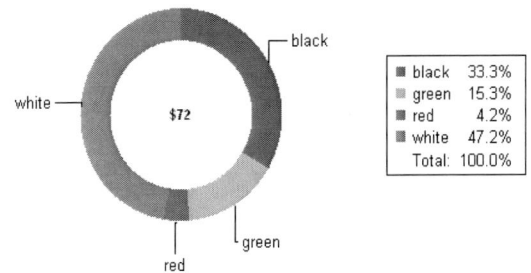

■ black	33.3%
■ green	15.3%
■ red	4.2%
■ white	47.2%
Total:	100.0%

black

white

$72

red

green

2. Match the color of each slice to its corresponding label.

a. **Select the slice labeled Black.**

b. **Right-click the slice and choose Format Pie Slice.**

c. From the Foreground Color drop-down list, **select the Black swatch, named 0, 0, 0.**

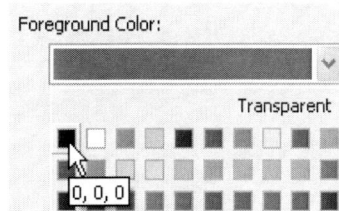

Foreground Color:

Transparent

0, 0, 0

d. **Click OK.**

e. **Select the slice labeled Green.**

f. **Display the Format Pie Slice dialog box.**

g. From the Foreground Color drop-down list, in the top row, **select the Green swatch, named 0, 128, 0, and click OK.**

h. **Select the slice labeled Red and display the Format Pie Slice dialog box.**

i. From the Foreground Color drop-down list, in the top row, **select the Red swatch, named 255, 0, 0, and click OK.**

j. **Select the slice labeled White and display the Format Pie Slice dialog box.**

k. From the Foreground Color drop-down list, in the top row, **select the White swatch, named 255, 255, 255, and click OK.**

Quantity by Helmet Color

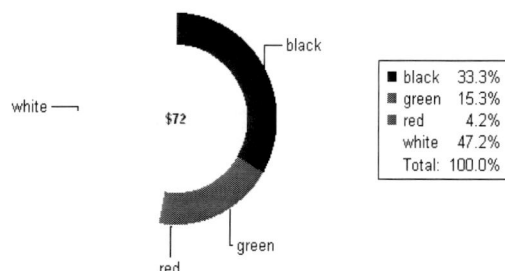

black

white

$72

■ black	33.3%
■ green	15.3%
■ red	4.2%
white	47.2%
Total:	100.0%

green

red

3. Change the border of the white slice to black.	a. To select the white slice, **click to the right of the White label.**

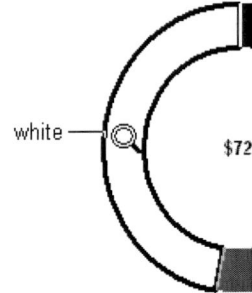

b. **Right-click and choose Format Pie Slice.**

c. **Select the Border tab.**

d. From the Color drop-down list, **select the Black swatch, named 0, 0, 0, and click OK.**

Quantity by Helmet Color

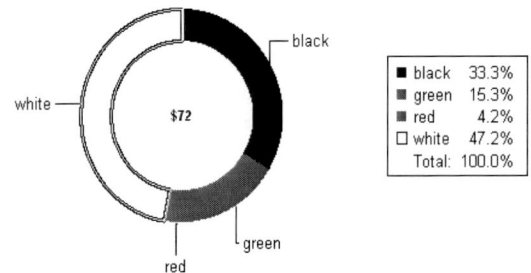

■	black	33.3%
■	green	15.3%
■	red	4.2%
☐	white	47.2%
	Total:	100.0%

4. **Turn off the display of labels.**	a. With the white slice still selected, **choose Chart→Chart Options.**
	b. **Select the Data Labels tab.**
	c. To turn off the display of labels, **uncheck the Show Labels check box.**

d. Uncheck the Show Pie Total check box and click OK.

Quantity by Helmet Color

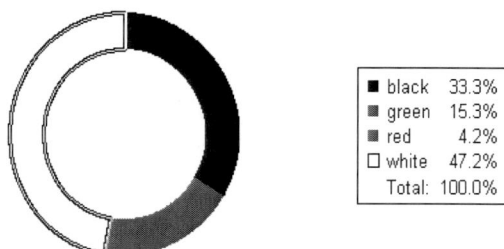

■ black	33.3%	
■ green	15.3%	
■ red	4.2%	
□ white	47.2%	
Total:	100.0%	

5. Save and close the Helmet Sales By Type report.

TOPIC D

Present a Chart by Group

When you want to create a chart based on grouped data, you may want to create a separate chart for each set of grouped data. In this topic, you will create a chart that reflects data for each data grouping in a grouped report.

You want to create a chart for a report that displays the first-quarter sales by month for each salesperson. The report is already grouped by salesperson, and displays their sales amounts for each month of the first quarter. Being able to present charts by group enables you to assess the data for each grouping.

How to Present a Chart by Group

Procedure Reference: Present a Chart by Group

To present a chart by group:

1. On the Design tab, begin creating a new chart by clicking the Insert Chart button and clicking in the desired Group Footer section.

2. On the Type tab, select the chart type of your choice.

3. On the Data tab, under Layout, verify that Advanced is selected.

4. Under Data, in the Available Fields list box, select the field on which you want to base your chart and click the top right arrow button to place the selected field in the associated list.

5. In the Available Fields list box, select the field you want to display on the chart and click the Show Value(s) bottom right arrow button to place the selected field in the Show Value(s) list.

6. If desired, on the Text tab, add a new title, subtitle, and/or footnote to your chart.

7. Click OK to create the chart.

8. If desired, to show each chart on its own page, in the Section Expert, select the section containing the chart, and check the New Page Before or New Page After check box.

ACTIVITY 7-4

Presenting a Chart by Group

Data Files:

*   Total Helmet Sales.rpt

Setup:

No files are open in Crystal Reports. The Start Page is displayed.

Scenario:

The Total Helmet Sales report contains a pie chart that summarizes the total helmet sales for four customers. You need to add a chart to each group that displays the percent of helmet sales by helmet type for each customer.

What You Do	How You Do It
1. In the Total Helmet Sales report, observe the chart.	a. **Open the Total Helmet Sales.rpt report.**
	b. **Click the Print Preview button.**
	c. **Observe the chart.** Notice that the chart displays the percent of helmet sales by helmet type for all customers.
2. **Begin creating a 3D pie chart in the Group Footer #1 section.**	a. **Select the Design tab.**
	b. On the Expert Tools toolbar, **click the Insert Chart button** .

c. To place the chart and display the Chart Expert, **click in the upper-left corner of the Group Footer #1 section.**

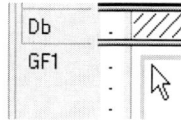

d. With the Chart Expert displayed, **select the Type tab.**

e. In the Choose Your Chart Type list, **select Pie.**

f. To make the pie three-dimensional, **check the Use Depth Effect check box.**

---

3. **Base the pie chart on the Product.Product Name field so that it displays the Orders_ Detail.Quantity field for each customer.**

a. **Select the Data tab.**

b. Under Layout, **verify that Advanced is selected.**

c. Under Data, in the Available Fields list box, **select Product.Product Name and click the top right arrow button.**

d. In the Available Fields list box, **select Orders_Detail.Quantity and click the bottom right arrow button.**

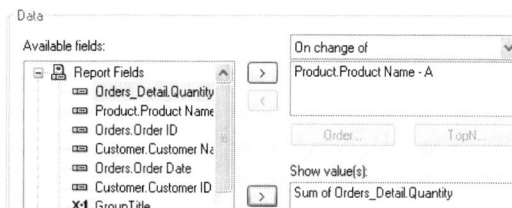

---

4. Title the chart *Helmet Types Sold*.

    a. **Select the Text tab.**

    b. Under Titles, to the right of Title, **uncheck Auto-Text and change the title to** *Helmet Types Sold*

    c. To create the chart, **click OK.**

5. Preview the report.

    a. **Select the Preview tab.**

    b. In the Group Tree, **select Alley Cat Cycles.**

    c. **Observe the chart.** Notice that the sub-title displays "For Alley Cat Cycles" and the chart shows the percentage of helmet types sold by that particular customer.

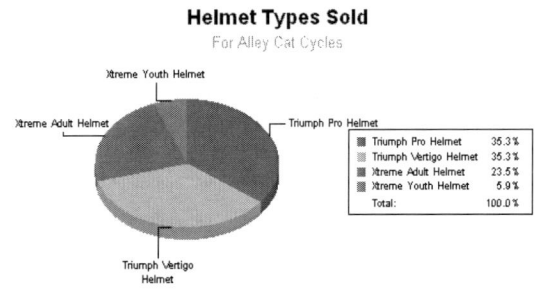

Helmet Types Sold
For Alley Cat Cycles

Triumph Pro Helmet	35.3 %
Triumph Vertigo Helmet	35.3 %
Xtreme Adult Helmet	23.5 %
Xtreme Youth Helmet	5.9 %
Total:	100.0 %

6. Save and close the Total Helmet Sales report.

Lesson 7 Follow-up

In this lesson, you created and modified pie charts. Graphical representations of data are often easier for users to comprehend quickly. By using charts, you can present data in a more readily accessible way, so users can identify trends and trouble spots.

1. **What types of charts will work best for your reports?**

2. **What types of formatting will you apply to customize your charts?**

LESSON 8
Distributing Data

Lesson Time
*45 minutes to 1 hour(s),
15 minutes*

Lesson Objectives:

In this lesson, you will distribute report data.

You will:

- Export a report to a PDF file.
- Export a report to Microsoft Excel.
- Export a report for use in Access.
- Export a report definition.
- Create mailing labels from a report.

Introduction

Once you have completed a report, you are ready to distribute the report to others. In this lesson, you will export report data so that you can distribute it to others.

People who need to view reports may not have Crystal Reports installed. By using the export options available in Crystal Reports, you can distribute a report or its associated database in a number of ways. Therefore, non-Crystal Reports users can access the reports you generate.

TOPIC A

Export to a PDF File

You may need to distribute a completed report to others who do not use Crystal Reports. In this topic, you will export report data to a PDF file.

You have created a report that you want to distribute to several coworkers who do not have Crystal Reports, or any database or spreadsheet applications. You can export the data in PDF format, which anyone could then view using the free Adobe Reader application.

Export Formats

When exporting data from Crystal Reports, you might lose some or all of the formatting. Crystal Reports attempts to preserve as much of the formatting as possible, based on the format type you choose.

List of Export Formats

You can export reports in the following formats:

- Adobe Acrobat (PDF)
- Crystal Reports (RPT)
- HTML 3.2
- HTML 4.0
- Microsoft Excel 97-2000 (XLS)
- Microsoft Excel 97-2000 - Data Only (XLS)
- Microsoft Word (RTF)
- Microsoft Word - Editable (RTF)
- ODBC
- Record Style - Columns With Spaces (REC)
- Record Style - Columns Without Spaces (REC)
- Report Definition (TXT)
- Rich Text Format (RTF)
- Separated Values (CSV)
- Tab-Separated Text (TTX)
- Text (TXT)
- XML

Report Export Options

As a report developer, when you choose File→Export→Report Export Options, you can set a default export format and associated options for the open report. So, when a user attempts to export the report, the export format you choose will be displayed by default. The user can either use the suggested format or modify it as needed.

PDF Files

Portable Document Format, or *PDF*, is an export file format that contains the report's data while still preserving the report's appearance. A PDF file can then be viewed using the free Adobe Reader application; however, because the PDF file's contents cannot be manipulated in Adobe Reader, the data and formatting integrity is therefore preserved.

How to Export to a PDF File

Procedure Reference: Export to a PDF File

To export a report from Crystal Reports to a PDF file:

1. Open the report to be exported.

2. Display the Export dialog box.
   - On the Standard toolbar, click the Export button.
   - Or, choose File→Export.

3. If necessary, from the Format drop-down list, select Adobe Acrobat (PDF).

4. If necessary, from the Destination drop-down list, select Disk File.

   🖉 To open the exported PDF file immediately, from the Destination drop-down list, select Application.

5. In the Export Options dialog box, select the desired page range to be included in the PDF file and click OK.

6. In the Choose Export File dialog box, navigate to where you want to save the PDF file, name the file, and click OK. The Exporting Records dialog box provides you with the export's progress.

7. If desired, preview the exported PDF file.

ACTIVITY 8-1

Exporting to PDF Format

Data Files:

- Order Summaries.rpt

Setup:

Adobe Reader, or another PDF reader, has been installed according to the setup instructions. No files are open in Crystal Reports. The Start Page is displayed.

Scenario:

You need to distribute the Order Summaries report to a number of your coworkers who need to view the report, but do not need to manipulate the report data. They do not have Crystal Reports installed on their computers.

What You Do	How You Do It
1. **Export the report to PDF format without opening it.**	a. **Open Order Summaries.rpt.**

b. **Observe the number of pages in the report.** Notice that it contains about 50 pages.

c. On the Standard toolbar, **click the Export button** [icon].

d. From the Format drop-down list, **verify that Adobe Acrobat (PDF) is selected.**

e. From the Destination drop-down list, **verify that Disk File is selected.**

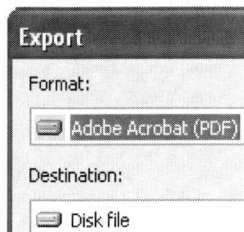

Export

Format:

[icon] Adobe Acrobat (PDF)

Destination:

[icon] Disk file

f. **Click OK.**

g. Under Page Range, **verify that the All option is selected and click OK.**

h. In the Choose Export File dialog box, in the Save In drop-down list, **navigate to C:\085517Data, verify that Order Summaries.pdf is the file name displayed, and click Save.**

[pushpin icon] If you are prompted to overwrite an existing file, click Yes.

2. Minimize Crystal Reports and open the Order Summaries.pdf file.

   a. Minimize the Crystal Reports window.

   b. Choose Start→My Computer and navigate to the C:\085517Data folder.

   c. Double-click Order Summaries.pdf.

   d. **Observe the report in Adobe Reader.** Notice that the formatting has been retained and that the PDF contains about 50 pages.

   e. **Exit Adobe Reader and minimize Windows Explorer.**

TOPIC B

Export to a Microsoft Excel File

You may need to distribute data from a completed report so others can access and modify the report's data. However, they may not have access to Crystal Reports. In this topic, you will export report data to a Microsoft Excel file.

You have created a report that includes data that several coworkers want to be able to access and modify for their own uses. Exporting the report to a Microsoft Excel file creates a copy of the report that others can access and modify using Excel.

How to Export to a Microsoft Excel File

Procedure Reference: Export to a Microsoft Excel File

To export a report to Microsoft Excel:

1. If necessary, open the report to be exported.

2. Display the Export dialog box.
   - On the Standard toolbar, click the Export button.
   - Or, choose File→Export.

3. From the Format drop-down list, select the desired Excel format.

4. From the Destination drop-down list, select the desired destination and click OK. The Excel Format Options dialog box is displayed.

5. Change the Excel Format Options as needed and click OK.

6. In the Select Export File dialog box, navigate to where you want to save the Excel file, name the file, and click OK. The Exporting Records dialog box provides you with the export's progress.

7.   If desired, preview the exported Excel file.

ACTIVITY 8-2

Exporting to Excel

Setup:

Microsoft Excel has been installed according to the setup instructions. Acrobat Reader has been closed and Windows Explorer has been minimized. The Order Summaries.rpt report is displayed on the Preview tab.

Scenario:

You need to distribute the Order Summaries report to a number of your coworkers who want to manipulate the report data for their own needs. They do not have Crystal Reports installed on their computers. However, they do have Microsoft Excel installed.

What You Do	How You Do It
1. **Export the report so that it immediately opens in Excel.**	a. On the Standard toolbar, **click the Export button.**
	b. From the Format drop-down list, **select Microsoft Excel 97-2000 (XLS).**
	c. From the Destination drop-down list, **select Application.**

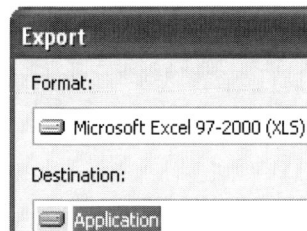

	d. **Click OK.**
	e. In the Excel Format Options dialog box, **click OK.**
	f. The report opens in Excel. **View the exported report within Excel.**

2.	Preview the exported report data in Excel.	a.	**Observe the report formatting.** Notice that the bold font style, field border, and the yellow background shading have been preserved.

4	Order Date	Order Amount
5	**7 Bikes For 7 Brothers (132.00)**	
6		
8	05/26/2004	$53.90
10		**$53.90**

		b.	**Observe the number of sheets in the Excel workbook.** All of the report data is included on a single sheet.

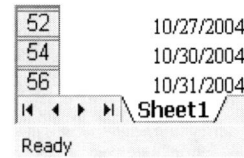

52	10/27/2004
54	10/30/2004
56	10/31/2004

|◀ ◀ ▶ ▶|\ **Sheet1** /

Ready

		c.	In Excel, **observe the title bar.** Because you exported the report directly to Excel, the file has been assigned a temporary file name.
3.	**Save the exported Excel file.**	a.	In Excel, **choose File→Save As.**
		b.	**Navigate to the 085517Data folder.**
		c.	In the File Name text box, **select the temporary file name and type** *Order Summaries*
		d.	**Click Save and exit Excel.**

TOPIC C

Export to an Access Database File

Another way to export report data is to export it for use with Microsoft Access. In this topic, you will export report data to an Access database file.

While Crystal Reports is a great report tool, it does not provide any direct access to an underlying database. If you need to access and modify the data displayed in your reports, you can easily export that data to a database. Then, you can modify the data in the exported database as necessary.

How to Export to an Access Database File

Procedure Reference: Export to an Access Database File

To export a report to an Access database:

1. If necessary, open the report to be exported.

2. Display the Export dialog box.
   - On the Standard toolbar, click the Export button.
   - Or, choose File→Export.

3. From the Format drop-down list, select ODBC and click OK. The ODBC Formats dialog box is displayed.

   🖉 ODBC stands for Open DataBase Connectivity. ODBC is a standard method for accessing databases.

4. From the list, select MS Access Database and click OK. The Select Database dialog box is displayed.

5. Under Directories, navigate to the folder where the database to which you want to export is located.

6. From the list under Database Name, select the desired database file and click OK. The Enter ODBC Table Name dialog box is displayed.

7. In the Table Name text box, if desired, type the appropriate name for the table and click OK. The Exporting Records dialog box provides you with the export's progress.

8. If desired, preview the exported data in Microsoft Access.

Report Items Exported to Access

Every object from the Crystal Reports report, including page number labels and group headers, is exported as a separate field, which can result in unwanted fields in the Access database. When creating a report specifically for export to a database, avoiding labels and other special fields will help give you the data without the extraneous items you may not want to include.

ACTIVITY 8-3

Exporting to an Access Database

Data Files:

- Employees-Orders.mdb

Setup:

Microsoft Access has been installed according to the setup instructions. Microsoft Excel has been closed. The Order Summaries.rpt report is displayed on the Preview tab.

Scenario:

You want to use the data in the Order Summaries report in an Access database so that you can access and modify the data itself.

What You Do	How You Do It
1. **Export the report data to a database.**	a. **Display the Export dialog box.**
	b. From the Format drop-down list, **select ODBC.**

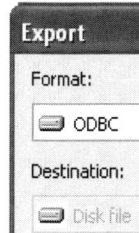

c. **Click OK.**

d. In the ODBC Formats dialog box, **select MS Access Database and click OK.**

e. In the Select Database dialog box, in the Database Name list box, **select Employees-Orders.mdb.**

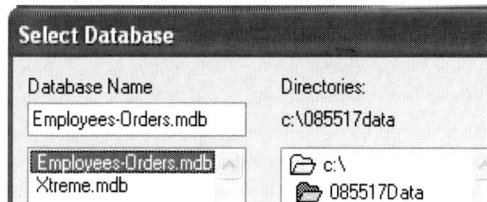

f. To display the Enter ODBC Table Name dialog box, **click OK.**

g. In the Table Name text box, **type *Orders***

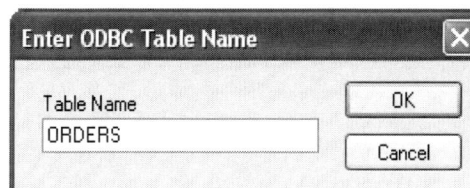

h. **Click OK.**

2. Preview the new table in Access.

    a. Choose Start→All Programs→Microsoft Office→Microsoft Office Access 2003.

    b. **Click the Open button**

    c. In the C:\085517Data folder, **open the Employees-Orders.mdb database file.**

    d. When prompted whether or not to block unsafe expressions, **click No.**

    e. When prompted with a security warning, **click Yes and click Open.**

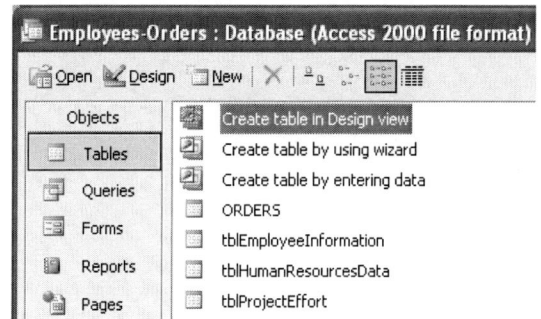

    f. With Tables displayed, **double-click ORDERS.**

---

3. Preview the exported table data and exit Access.

    a. **Observe the column headings.** Notice that there is one column for each report section that contained a field.

    b. **Observe the data.** Notice that no font, field, or background formatting has been included.

    c. **Observe the sixth column, DE_Orders_ Order_Amount.** Notice that the amounts are not formatted as currency. The report provides the numeric formatting.

    d. **Click the Close button** to exit Access.

    e. **Save your changes** before exiting Access.

TOPIC D

Export a Report Definition

When you are sharing report data with others, you may also want to share information about how the report was created, such as formatting options and formulas used in the report. In this topic, you will create a file detailing this type of report information.

Creating a report definition provides a single file that contains detailed information concerning your report. The report definition serves both as a troubleshooting tool and a paper backup, and it is simple to create.

Report Definition

When you create a report, you might find that you want to document how the report was designed. You can do that by creating a *report definition file*. It is a text file that contains the details of the design of a report, such as the fields included in the report, the formulas that have been created in the report, and the objects in each section.

How to Export a Report Definition

Procedure Reference: Create a Report Definition

To create a report definition:

1. If necessary, open the report for which you want to create a definition.

2. Display the Export dialog box.
    *   On the Standard toolbar, click the Export button.
    *   Or, choose File→Export.

3. From the Format drop-down list, select Report Definition.

4. From the Destination drop-down list, select the desired destination and click OK. If you selected Application, the report definition file will open in Notepad. If you selected Disk File, the Choose Export File dialog box is displayed.
    a. If necessary, navigate to where you want to save the file.
    b. If necessary, in the File Name text box, type a name for your report definition.
    c. Click Save.

5. If desired, preview the exported report definition file.

    🖈 Formulas that are buried in group header names and in conditional formulas do not display in the report definition file unless the user moves a copy of all those formulas into the report somewhere. When all formulas are needed in the report definition file, buried formulas must be added to the report. They can be suppressed so that they do not display in the preview copy.

ACTIVITY 8-4

Creating a Report Definition

Setup:

The Order Summaries.rpt report is displayed on the Preview tab.

Scenario:

The Order Summaries report is a good example of the type of reports you will continue to create. Therefore, you want to save information on the design of that report for future reference.

What You Do	How You Do It
1. Create a report definition file for Order Summaries.rpt.	a. Display the Export dialog box.
	b. From the Format drop-down list, **select Report Definition (TXT).**
	c. From the Destination drop-down list, **select Application.**
	Export
	Format:
	Report Definition (TXT)
	Destination:
	Application
	d. **Click OK.**
2. Preview the report definition and exit Notepad.	a. The report definition file is opened in Notepad. **Maximize Notepad and scroll through the report.**
	b. **Observe the report definition contents.** Notice that the report definition provides details about the File, Record Sort Fields, Group Sort Fields, Formulas, and Sections contained within the report.
	c. **Exit Notepad.**
3. Close the Orders Summaries report.	

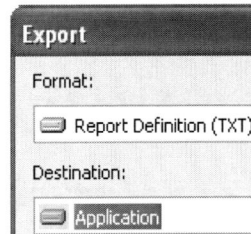

TOPIC E

Create Mailing Labels

When you need to distribute anything using conventional mail, you can use Crystal Reports to generate your mailing labels. In this topic, you will use the Mailing Labels Report Wizard to create a report for generating mailing labels.

By using the Mailing Labels Report Wizard in Crystal Reports, you can create a report that is formatted to print on any size mailing labels. The wizard makes it quick and easy to produce professional-looking mailing labels.

Report Creation Wizard

Crystal Reports provides you with four Report Creation Wizards from which to choose.

Wizard	Helps Create
Standard Report	Typical reports.
Cross-Tab Report	Reports with a summarized grid.
Mailing Labels Report	Reports with multiple columns.
OLAP Cube Report	Reports that contain a summarized grid based on an OLAP data source.

Limitations of Report Creation Wizards

With the exception of special needs, such as creating mailing labels, using Report Creation Wizards is not generally recommended for report creation. The tool is very useful for the novice Crystal Reports user, but it has some limitations. It is not possible to return to the Report Creation Wizard once a report is finalized (only the template version of it remains behind). Therefore, users are encouraged to learn how to use the standard built-in features rather than rely upon the wizard.

How to Create Mailing Labels

Procedure Reference: Create Mailing Labels

To create mailing labels:

1. Display the Mailing Labels Report Creation Wizard.
   - On the Start Page, under New Reports, click Mailing Label Report Wizard.
   - Or, choose File→New→Mailing Label Report.

2. On the Data page of the Mailing Labels Report Creation Wizard, expand the Create New Connection category.

3. Expand the Database Files folder, select the desired data source, and click Open.

4. Below the selected data source, add the tables that contain the fields you want to include in the report and click Next.

5. If desired, modify the automatic links and click Next.

6. On the Fields page, add the fields you want to include in the report and click Next. Each field you add will display on its own line.

7. On the Label page, select the Mailing Label Type, dimensions, and printing options, and click Next.

8. If desired, on the Record Selection page, select an optional subset of data to display.

9. Click Finish to create the report with mailing labels.

10. In the report, add or modify any of the fields as desired to finalize the label layout.

ACTIVITY 8-5

Creating Mailing Labels

Setup:

No files are open in Crystal Reports. The Start Page is displayed.

Scenario:

The human resources manager has a brochure that she wants to mail to all employees. She needs you to assist her with the mailing.

What You Do	How You Do It
1. **Begin creating the mailing labels based on the Employee and Employee Addresses tables from the Xtreme database.**	a. On the Start Page, under New Reports, **click Mailing Label Report Wizard.**
	b. In the Available Data Sources list box, **expand the Database Files folder.**
	c. **Select Xtreme.mdb and click Open.**
	d. Under Xtreme.mdb, **expand Tables.**
	e. **Add the Employee and Employee Addresses tables.**

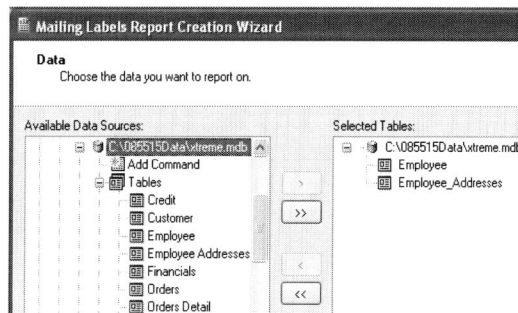

Mailing Labels Report Creation Wizard

Data
Choose the data you want to report on.

Available Data Sources:
- C:\085515Data\xtreme.mdb
  - Add Command
  - Tables
    - Credit
    - Customer
    - Employee
    - Employee Addresses
    - Financials
    - Orders
    - Orders Detail

Selected Tables:
- C:\085515Data\xtreme.mdb
  - Employee
  - Employee_Addresses

f. **Click Next.**

g. **Observe the linked tables.** Notice that the common Employee ID fields have been linked automatically.

h. **Click Next.**

2. From the Employee table, **add the First Name field.**

   a. In the Available Fields list box, **select First Name.**

   b. **Click the Add arrow button.**

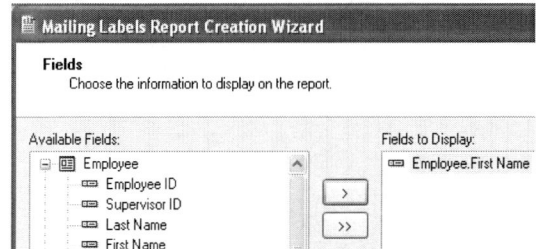

   c. **Observe the Last Name field.** Notice that it is not being added. Since each field you add using the wizard will appear on its own line, you will manually add the Last Name field later.

3. From the Employee Addresses table, **add the Address1, Address2, and City fields.**

   a. In the Available Fields list box, **scroll down and expand the Employee_ Addresses table.**

   b. **Add the Address1, Address2, and City fields.**

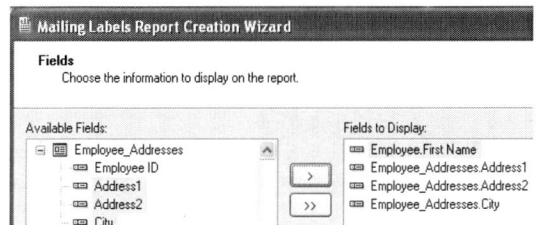

   c. **Observe the Region and Postal Code fields.** Notice that they are not being added. Again, you will manually add these fields later.

   d. **Click Next.**

4. Set the label type and save the file.

    a. From the Mailing Label Type drop-down list, **select Address (Avery 5160).**

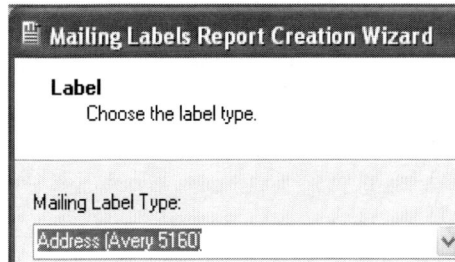

> **Mailing Labels Report Creation Wizard**
>
> **Label**
>   Choose the label type.
>
> Mailing Label Type:
> Address (Avery 5160)

    b. **Click Finish.**

    c. **Save the report as *Labels***

---

5. You need to fix the labels by using formulas so the entire name and city, region, and zip code are displayed. What formula would you write to concatenate the First Name and Last Name fields with a space between the fields?

---

6. **Create a formula that concatenates the First Name and Last Name fields.**

    a. In the Field Explorer, **create a formula named *EmployeeName***

    b. To concatenate the First Name and Last Name fields, in the Formula Text window, **type {Employee.First Name}&" "&{Employee.Last Name}**

    c. **Check the formula for errors.**

    d. **Save and close the formula.**

LESSON 8

7. **Create a formula that concatenates the City, Region, and Postal Code fields.**

   a. In the Field Explorer, **create a formula named *CityRegionZip***

   b. To concatenate the City, Region, and Postal Code fields, in the Formula Text window, **type** `{Employee_Addresses.City}&", "&{Employee_Addresses.Region}⇒ &" "&{Employee_Addresses.Postal Code}`

   > 📌 There should be a comma and space between the City and Region fields and a space between the Region and Postal Code fields.

   c. **Check the formula for errors.**

   d. **Save and close the formula.**

8. **Replace the First Name and City fields with the Employee Name and CityRegionZip formula fields.**

   a. **Select the Design tab.**

   b. **Delete the First Name field and replace it with the Employee Name field.**

   c. **Delete the City field and replace it with the CityRegionZip field.**

Da	@EmployeeName
Db	Address1
Dc	Address2
Dd	@CityRegionZip

   d. **Preview the report.**

   e. Some of the addresses are missing an @CityRegionZip field because some of the Region fields in the database are empty. Some of the postal code data is cut off. **Widen the CityRegionZip field to the 2.5″ mark.**

   Tim Smith
   30301 - 166th Ave. N.E.
   Apt #3D
   North Vancouver, BC V3K 2G9

9. **Save the report as *All Employee Labels* and close the report.**

Lesson 8 Follow-up

In this lesson, you explored a number of ways to distribute report data to other users. Now when you need to share report data, you will be able to provide the data to your audience in a useful format, regardless of whether or not they have Crystal Reports.

1. **In what format will you export reports?**

2. **Do you have reports for which you will create a report definition? If so, what types of reports are they?**

Follow-up

In this course, you have practiced the skills needed to build basic list and group reports. Now you can take the information you have locked away in a database and use Crystal Reports to create reports that display exactly the detail you need. You can sort, filter, group, format, and enhance the data in your reports, as needed, and then distribute those reports in the appropriate format to the people who need them.

What's Next?

Crystal Reports XI: Level 1 is the first course in this series. Students who want to learn advanced features can take *Crystal Reports XI: Level 2*.

LESSON LABS

Due to classroom setup constraints, some labs cannot be keyed in sequence immediately following their associated lesson. Your instructor will tell you whether your labs can be practiced immediately following the lesson or whether they require separate setup from the main lesson content.

LESSON 1 LAB 1

Creating a Report

Activity Time:

20 minutes to 30 minutes

Setup:

In order for the provided report files to connect to the database, if you have not done so already, you may need to:

1. Create a new folder on your C: drive named 085517Data

2. Locate the xtreme.mdb database located at C:\Program Files\Business Objects\Crystal Reports 11\Samples\en (this file should have been provided with your Crystal Reports software).

3. Move the xtreme.mdb database into the newly created 085517Data folder.

Scenario:

You work for a company that sells bicycles and equipment, and the human resources manager has asked you to present basic employee information from the Xtreme database. You need to create a report.

🖈 You can compare your results to Solutions\Employee Information Solution.rpt.

---

1. **Create a blank report using the Employee and Employee Addresses tables in the Xtreme.mdb database.**

---

2. From the Employee table, **add the Employee ID, Last Name, First Name, and Hire Date fields to the report.** From the Employee Addresses table, **add the Region and Postal Code fields to the report.**

3. **Change the field label for the Employee ID field to** *Employee #* **and change the field label for the Postal Code field to** *Zip Code*.

4. **Add a report title of your choice that displays in the font size and style desired, and center the title between the margins.**

5. If necessary, **align and resize the fields as desired.**

6. **Preview the report.**

7. **Save and close the report.**

LESSON 2 LAB 1

Sorting and Filtering Data

Data Files:

- Employee List.rpt

Setup:

In order for the provided report files to connect to the database, if you have not done so already, you may need to:

1. Create a new folder on your C: drive named 085517Data

2. Locate the xtreme.mdb database located at C:\Program Files\Business Objects\Crystal Reports 11\Samples\en (this file should have been provided with your Crystal Reports software).

3. Move the xtreme.mdb database into the newly created 085517Data folder.

Scenario:

You work for a company that sells bicycles and related equipment. You created a report named Employee List for the human resources manager. The report needs to be sorted alphabetically. Also, the human resources manager wants a list of those employees who live in France's Bas-Rhin region immediately.

🔖 You can compare your results to Employee List Solution.rpt.

1. **Open the Employee List.rpt report.**

2. Sort the report by last name in alphabetical order.

3. Filter the report using refreshed data so that only the employees in Bas-Rhin are displayed.

4. Save and close the report.

LESSON 3 LAB 1

Updating a Report with Grouping

Data Files:

- Employee Orders By Region.rpt

- Solutions\Employee Orders By Region Solution.rpt

Setup:

In order for the provided report files to connect to the database, if you have not done so already, you may need to:

1. Create a new folder on your C: drive named 085517Data

2. Locate the xtreme.mdb database located at C:\Program Files\Business Objects\Crystal Reports 11\Samples\en (this file should have been provided with your Crystal Reports software).

3. Move the xtreme.mdb database into the newly created 085517Data folder.

Scenario:

You have created a basic report named Employee Orders By Region that includes the order amount for each employee and the region where each is located. However, the reports needs to be better organized so the information will be more meaningful to your audience.

🖈 You can compare your results to Solutions\Employee Orders By Region Solution.rpt.

1. Open the Employee Orders By Region.rpt report.

2. Group the report in ascending order by the Employee ID field, and preview the report.

🖈 Some of the fields for particular records are blank because they do not contain any data.

3. Specify that the data for each group remain together on one page when possible, and specify that the group header for each group displays at the top of each page.

4. Insert a summary total for the Employee.Employee ID group that sums the Order Amount field, and insert a grand total.

5. Format the group header for each group as desired.

6. Filter the report to display only those groups whose Order Amount total is more than $700,000.

7. Remove the filter you just created, and display the top four groups in terms of their Order Amount totals.

8. Save the changes to the report.

9. If desired, **compare your results with the sample file Employee Orders By Region Solution.rpt.**

10. **Close all reports.**

LESSON 4 LAB 1

Creating Formulas

Data Files:

- Credit Authorizations.rpt

Setup:

In order for the provided report files to connect to the database, if you have not done so already, you may need to:

1. Create a new folder on your C: drive named 085517Data

2. Locate the xtreme.mdb database located at C:\Program Files\Business Objects\Crystal Reports 11\Samples\en (this file should have been provided with your Crystal Reports software).

3. Move the xtreme.mdb database into the newly created 085517Data folder.

Scenario:

You have created a report for the credit manager named Credit Authorizations, which includes customer credit IDs and amounts. You need to make a few changes to it so that the users will be able to quickly reference a specific credit authorization number as soon as they open the report.

🖈 You can compare your results to Solutions\Credit Authorizations Solution.rpt.

1. Open Credit Authorizations.rpt.

2. Create a formula field named *Contact Name* that concatenates the Customer.Contact First Name, Customer.Contact Last Name, and Customer.Phone fields. There should be a space between each field.

3. Place the Contact Name field in the Group Footer to the right of the Sum Of Credit.Amount field and resize it as needed.

4. Edit the Contact Name field so that it includes a comma after Customer.Contact Last Name.

5. Create a parameter field using the following information:
   - The field should be named Authorization and prompt the user to select the credit authorization number.
   - The Value Field should be Credit Authorization Number.
   - The default list should include all the database values.
   - Resize and place the parameter formula at approximately the 6″ mark in the Page Header section.

6. Apply bold formatting to the parameter formula field.

7. Create a selection formula where Credit.Credit Authorization Number equals the Authorization parameter formula.

8. Preview the report using a value of your choice.

9. Save the report.

10. If desired, **compare your report to the file Credit Authorizations Solution.rpt.**

11. Close all open files.

LESSON 5 LAB 1

Formatting a Report

Data Files:

- Sales By Region.rpt

Setup:

In order for the provided report files to connect to the database, if you have not done so already, you may need to:

1. Create a new folder on your C: drive named 085517Data

2. Locate the xtreme.mdb database located at C:\Program Files\Business Objects\Crystal Reports 11\Samples\en (this file should have been provided with your Crystal Reports software).

3. Move the xtreme.mdb database into the newly created 085517Data folder.

Scenario:

You work for a company that sells bicycles and equipment. You have just finished building a report named Sales By Region. You need to format the report to make the data easier to interpret at a glance.

You can compare your results to Solutions\Sales By Region Solution.rpt.

---

1. Open the report Sales By Region.rpt.

---

2. Remove some of the excess white space that appears between the report records.

---

3. Add a colored border of your choice to a field of your choice.

---

4. Add a single box around both the Employee ID and Region fields and labels in the Group Header #1 and #2 sections. Move the fields, labels, and box as necessary.

---

5. Change the background color of any field to a color of your choice.

---

6. Add the page number to the bottom of each page.

---

7. Increase the report's left margin to .5".

---

8. Preview the report.

---

9. Compare your results with the sample file Sales By Region Solution.rpt.

---

10. Close all open reports, saving if prompted.

LESSON 6 LAB 1

Enhancing a Report

Data Files:

- Addresses.rpt

Setup:

In order for the provided report files to connect to the database, if you have not done so already, you may need to:

1. Create a new folder on your C: drive named 085517Data

2. Locate the xtreme.mdb database located at C:\Program Files\Business Objects\Crystal Reports 11\Samples\en (this file should have been provided with your Crystal Reports software).

3. Move the xtreme.mdb database into the newly created 085517Data folder.

Scenario:

You work for a company that sells bicycles and equipment. You have created a report named Addresses. You want to indicate that the report is from your company and provide users with an easy way to send you an email.

🖈 You can compare your results to Solutions\Addresses Solution.rpt.

---

1. **Open the report Addresses.rpt.**

---

2. **Specify that the Address2 and @CityRegionZip fields not display when their contents are blank.**

---

3. At the guideline in the Page Header section, **place the Xtreme.bmp graphic so that you can modify it directly from within Crystal Reports.**

---

4. **Modify the Xtreme.bmp graphic so that its background is white, instead of black. Use the Paint swatches at the bottom of the window to specify a white color, then click the black areas using the Fill With Color tool.**

---

5. **Set the section containing the Xtreme.bmp graphic so that the following sections overlay it.**

---

6. In the Report Footer section, **insert a text object that reads *Have questions? Click here!***

---

7. **Resize and format the text object so it appears as a link.**

8. **Create a link for the text object to your email address.**

   🖈 If you do not have an email address, use jdoe@example.com.

9. **Preview the report.**

10. **Test the link and cancel any open dialog or message boxes. Close any email programs that may launch.**

11. **Compare your results with the sample file Addresses Solution.rpt.**

12. **Close all open reports, saving if prompted.**

LESSON 7 LAB 1

Creating a Pie Chart

Data Files:

• Sales By Salesperson.rpt

Setup:

In order for the provided report files to connect to the database, if you have not done so already, you may need to:

1. Create a new folder on your C: drive named 085517Data

2. Locate the xtreme.mdb database located at C:\Program Files\Business Objects\Crystal Reports 11\Samples\en (this file should have been provided with your Crystal Reports software).

3. Move the xtreme.mdb database into the newly created 085517Data folder.

Scenario:

You work for a company that sells bicycles and equipment. You have created a report named Sales By Salesperson that summarizes first-quarter sales by salesperson. You need to chart each salesperson's contribution as a percentage of the total sales. In addition, for each salesperson, you need to create a chart that displays his or her sales amounts for the quarter.

🖈 You can compare your results to Solutions\Sales By Salesperson Solution.rpt.

1. **Open Sales By Salesperson.rpt.**

2. Create a pie chart based on the @Name field that shows the Sum Of Sheet1_ .Sales data.

3. Change the chart title to *First-Quarter Sales*.

4. Create additional pie charts for each salesperson that shows the value of his or her sales data by month.

5. Format the pie slice labels to display at a size of 10 pts and modify any other label formatting as desired.

6. Change the color of each pie slice.

7. Remove the chart legends.

8. Resize the chart as necessary.

9. Format each group so that the data and associated chart are displayed on its own page.

10. If desired, **compare your report to the file Sales By Salesperson Solution.rpt.**

11. Close all open reports, saving if prompted.

LESSON 8 LAB 1

Exporting Reports and Creating Report Definitions

Activity Time:

10 minutes to 20 minutes

Data Files:

* Employee Data.rpt

Setup:

In order for the provided report files to connect to the database, if you have not done so already, you may need to:

1. Create a new folder on your C: drive named 085517Data

2. Locate the xtreme.mdb database located at C:\Program Files\Business Objects\Crystal Reports 11\Samples\en (this file should have been provided with your Crystal Reports software).

3. Move the xtreme.mdb database into the newly created 085517Data folder.

Scenario:

You work for a company that sells bicycles and equipment. You have created a report in Crystal Reports named Employee Data. You need to share this report with several executives who do not have Crystal Reports or any database or spreadsheet applications. You also need to distribute it to members of the human resources department so that they can view the material and make modifications to it using spreadsheet or database applications. You plan to create additional reports that are similar to this one, so you want to document the details of the report's structure and components.

> 🖊 You can compare your results to Solutions\Employee Data Solution.pdf, Employee Data Solution.xls, and Report Definition Solution.txt.

1. **Open the file Employee Data.rpt.**

2. **Export the report to PDF format, saving the new file to the 085517Data folder.**

3. **Export the report to Excel 97-2000 format, saving the new file to the 085517Data folder.**

4. **Export the report to Access format, saving it to the Employees-Orders.mdb file, and naming the table *EMPLOYEES*.**

5. **Export a report definition to Notepad.**

6. **Save the report definition file as *Report Definition.txt*.**

7. **Exit Notepad, saving if prompted.**

8. **Exit Crystal Reports.**

SOLUTIONS

Lesson 1

Activity 1-3

2. On the Preview tab, what do you notice about the field placeholders?

   a) The field placeholders remain displayed.

   ✓ b) The field placeholders display records from the database.

   c) Only a single row of database records is displayed.

   d) The field placeholders only display pound signs, #####.

4. Approximately how many pages are in the report?

   a) 2

   b) 10

   c) 25

   ✓ d) 35

5. According to the Status bar, how many records are included in the report?

   a) 253

   b) 270

   c) 1505

   ✓ d) 2191

Lesson 2

Activity 2-1

3. What is the correct amount for Mad Mountain Bikes' Order # 2,783?

   a) $1,781.25

   b) $67.80

   ✓ c) $1,439.55

   d) $15.50

SOLUTIONS

5. **What happened when you clicked Find Next?**

   a) The string was found.

   ✓ b) The string was not found.

   c) Multiple records were found.

   d) The Search Expert was displayed.

7. **What is the correct amount for City Cyclists' Order # 1,092?**

   ✓ a) $42.00

   b) $62.33

   c) $3,884.25

   d) $6,682.98

Activity 2-2

2. **Which company placed the largest order?**

   a) Bikes for Tykes

   b) The Great Bike Shop

   ✓ c) Insane Cycle

   d) Wheels and Stuff

5. **What was the date of the most recent order for Alley Cat Cycles?**

   a) 5/26/04

   b) 6/21/04

   ✓ c) 4/9/05

   d) 3/7/05

Activity 2-3

3. **According to the Status bar, how many orders were placed for more than $500?**

   a) 1,307

   ✓ b) 1,281

   c) 100

   d) 2,191

5. **According to the Status bar, how many orders were placed for more than $5,000?**

   ✓ a) 296

   b) 1,320

   c) 2,735

   d) 0

Lesson 3

Activity 3-2

4. What is the order amount summary total for Bikes For Tykes?

    a) $48,086.23

✓ b) $35,376.01

    c) $47,225.53

    d) $959.70

6. What is the grand total for all customers?

    a) $50,512.26

    b) $989.55

    c) $2,939.85

✓ d) $3,982,734.36

Lesson 4

Activity 4-6

3. How many customers from MA and CA placed orders in January 2004?

    a) 2

    b) 3

✓ c) 8

    d) 9

Activity 4-7

4. Is it necessary to place the parameter field within the layout for it to function?

No, the parameter field does not have to appear within the layout, but may be placed in the layout if you want it to display in the report itself.

Lesson 5

Activity 5-1

3. **What happens when you try to move the section boundary up more?**

   You cannot because the field's boundary prevents it.

   Why can't the section's white space be further decreased?

   You cannot make the section smaller because the field and the vertical guideline are in the way.

Lesson 8

Activity 8-5

5. **You need to fix the labels by using formulas so the entire name and city, region, and zip code are displayed. What formula would you write to concatenate the First Name and Last Name fields with a space between the fields?**

   {Employee.First Name}&" "&{Employee.Last Name}

GLOSSARY

ascending order
Records are sorted from smallest to largest (that is, 1 to 9, A to Z).

attribute formula
Requires additional information to specify the formatting properties and uses an If-Then-Else statement.

boolean formula
Any formula that returns a true/false value.

border
A visible representation of a field or other text object's boundaries.

comparison operator
A statement you can use to compare data in a field that has a fixed value with the content of another field.

components
The parts of the formula.

concatenate
To string fields together—for example, combining the first and last name fields to show a full name.

conditional formatting
Formatting that is applied based on specific criteria.

criteria
The rules on which a decision is based.

database
A collection of related data divided into specific categories.

descending order
Records are sorted from largest to smallest (that is, 9 to 1, Z to A).

filter
Allows you to display certain records based on specific criteria.

formula
An equation that performs operations on data.

group
A collection of related data based on a selected field or formula that displays in a desired order.

index
A list of pointers to records in a table, sorted by value(s) in one or more fields of that table.

link
A common field between two or more tables that is used to connect the tables in a relational database.

natural order
The order in which data is entered into a database.

null
The absence of data. (Null should not be confused with zero.)

OLE
(Object Linking and Embedding) Allows you to link or embed an object, such as a spreadsheet, video clip, or text document into a document called the container application.

operators
The actions you can use in your formulas to specify the type of calculation that you want to perform.

GLOSSARY

PDF

(Portable Document Format) A file format that preserves a file's appearance as it existed in the authoring application.

relational database

A database in which data is stored in a structure of rows and columns, usually called tables, and in which data can be shared among tables through established relationships.

report definition file

A text file that contains the details of the design of a report, such as the tables included in the report, the formulas that have been created in the report, and the objects in each section.

selection formula

A filter used to limit the data included in a report.

special fields

System-generated fields, such as Page Number, Print Date, File Path And Name, and Report Comments, that can be added to any section in a report, such as the Page Header and Page Footer sections, to provide information about that report.

summary operation

A type of mathematical function that you can use to summarize the data in a report.

syntax

The rules that you must follow when organizing the components of a formula.

INDEX

INDEX